Focus on Dyspraxia:
Let's move on

CHRISTINE MACINTYRE

A NASEN Publication

Published in 2003

ISBN 1 901485 59 5

Published by NASEN.
NASEN is a registered charity. Charity No. 1007023.
NASEN is a company limited by guarantee, registered in England and Wales.
Company No. 2674379.

Further copies of this book and details of NASEN's many other publications may be obtained from the NASEN Bookshop at its registered office:
NASEN House, 4/5 Amber Business Village, Amber Close, Amington, Tamworth, Staffs. B77 4RP.
Tel: 01827 311500 Fax: 01827 313005 Email: welcome@nasen.org.uk
Web site: www.nasen.org.uk

Cover design by Mark Procter.
Typeset by J. C. Typesetting.
Typeset in Times and printed in the United Kingdom by Stowes (Stoke-on-Trent).

FOCUS ON DYSPRAXIA:
LET'S MOVE ON

Contents

FOCUS ON DYSPRAXIA: LET'S MOVE ON

Introduction

Dyspraxia is a specific learning difficulty. This means that while children with dyspraxia have many strengths, one aspect of their development, in this case the ability to plan and carry out effective and efficient movements, lets them down, significantly hindering their progress. And because all aspects of development are interdependent (Bee, 1999), this movement deficit has a knock-on effect on social, emotional and intellectual development as well. The good news is that while as yet there is no 'cure' for dyspraxia, every child, adolescent or adult can be helped. The label need not stick (Caan, 1998). It is never too late for support to be effective, especially when it is positive, i.e. beginning from the person's areas of strength and whenever possible, building on the things they want to be able to do. More and more children are presenting with specific learning difficulties (Keen, 2001). While this is distressing and raises many questions as to why this should be, it also results in more parents, teachers and many of those affected by dyspraxia being keen to learn about the condition and how to ameliorate its effects. Hopefully this will result in the most appropriate kind of support being offered at the most appropriate moment and for the correct amount of time.

Children are born with dyspraxia. They do not catch it from a virus or from anyone else. The after-effects of flu or operations can mimic dyspraxia because the weakness leaves people feeling 'inarticulate' in a movement sense – e.g. in having to think how to go down stairs, needing a banister to get there and feeling exhausted by the effort. But this will pass, it is not dyspraxia. Nor is dyspraxia a progressive illness such as muscular dystrophy. No one dies of dyspraxia, although without support and understanding, some people can be left with severe depression. This is due to not being able to do the things they wish to do and feeling frustrated, even worthless as a result.

Although dyspraxia is not life-threatening, and this must be a huge comfort to everyone concerned, it is disabling and as soon as possible strategies to help must be put in place. Movement underlies most activities of daily living as well as those that are necessary to succeed in school and so the effects of having dyspraxia are widespread. Adults must therefore be able to recognise the early signs and seek appropriate help.

The transitory nature of movement means that assessing it is quite complicated. Often parents say, 'We know there is something wrong, but what?' and they need time and patience and knowledge about the analysis of movement if they are to give an adequate appraisal. Once this is learned, parents and teachers can do a great deal to minimise or bypass the effects of the condition. Preparing timetables to reduce the stress of remembering can help planning and organising difficulties, while giving children who find writing tiring and challenging a laptop, are just two examples of strategies to help.

There are a number of difficulties that are all part of dyspraxia, e.g. a poor short-term memory which leads to difficulty in following instructions, as well as the more obvious movement difficulties such as not being able to spread toast or do up buttons or catch a ball. Some children have several difficulties while others have only one or two. Dyspraxia may also be mild or severe. It may co-occur with another specific learning difficulty such as dyslexia or ADHD (attention deficit hyperactivity disorder). This makes accurate diagnosis tricky and is one reason why children with similar symptoms can be given different labels. A second is that those making a formal diagnosis may first identify difficulties that are most familiar to them (Keen, 2001). Everyone must look beyond the label to assess the whole child (Macintyre & Deponio, 2003).

Assessment leading to appropriate support is essential, for without it the increased expectations placed upon children as they grow and become more independent, mean that their difficulties may increase or they may find fewer educational or employment options open to them. To prevent this happening, families and teachers need to understand dyspraxia and what it means for those who have it. They also need to know how best they can help.

The book explains what dyspraxia is; it gives real life case studies to show the effects of living with the condition; and it offers tried and tested ways to support those who are affected so that they may fulfil the potential they undoubtedly have. It considers the overlapping difficulties shared by dyspraxia and the other specific learning difficulties. This should help to clarify any diagnosis and ensure that the correct one has been given. It also suggests how children with different needs can be helped together in groups. This means they can make friends and share their progress, so avoiding the social isolation that could so easily become a feature of their lives.

Chapter 1
Dyspraxia: an overview

In this first chapter, five questions are addressed. They are 'What is dyspraxia?' 'How many people are affected?' 'What are the first signs?' 'Do people grow out of it?' and 'Should children with dyspraxia have a label?' These are considered together in this overview and issues arising from them are discussed in more detail in subsequent chapters.

Question 1: What is dyspraxia?

'Dyspraxia is a significant impairment in the motor aspect of development. It has associated problems with language and thought.'

(The Dyspraxia Foundation (2000) Praxis makes Perfect. Newsletter of the D.F.)

The name 'dyspraxia' (*dys* meaning faulty and *praxis* meaning use of the body) is the term most often used in schools, colleges and universities today to describe children and students who have difficulty moving efficiently and effectively in different environments. It sits alongside dyslexia, dysgraphia and dyscalculia as one of a group of specific learning difficulties. Many teachers are used to these terms now and are working hard to recognise and mitigate the implications of the different 'dys'-abilities where poor movement is a key factor. This involves them in observing and assessing the different types of movement to find exactly where the children's difficulties lie. They then prepare the most appropriate strategies to support them. This is a complex undertaking because moving well requires a number of underlying competences to be in place. These are:

- Knowing what to do, i.e. having a visual image of the chosen movement (Ideation).
- Being able to analyse that movement and plan so that the discrete parts happen in sequence (Analysis).
- Having the physical attributes, e.g. enough strength or length of limb (Body build).
- Having the perceptual abilities, i.e. being able to integrate sensory information to guide planning (Knowing what to do when and where to make it happen).
- Having the movement abilities, e.g. co-ordination, balance and rhythmic awareness to carry the movement out (Execution).
- Being able to pay attention to learn (Attention and concentration).
- Being able to remember and so build on previous experience (Short-term memory).
- Being able to transfer movement skills from one environment to another with easy adaptation (Habituation).
- Being able to use the feedback from one attempt to improve the next.

If there is a deficit in a cluster of these competences, dyspraxia may be cited as the cause.

In schools, the term 'dyspraxia' is often used to describe movement difficulties even though the children have not been tested by any 'outside' experts (Henderson & Barnett, 1998). Perhaps this is due to the difficulty in gaining referrals to psychologists or physiotherapists or perhaps teachers and parents working together recognise the wealth of information they have about how a child copes or fails to cope across a spectrum of activities. Local 'dyspraxia groups' are being formed and many interested researchers and other experienced adults are willing to share strategies that have helped their children. Given this kind of ongoing, 'local' advice, many teachers, especially those supporting the youngest children, prefer to do without the label which could result from a formal diagnosis. They are afraid of making the children feel 'different'. This could also act against the ethos of inclusion which teachers are striving to promote (Scottish Executive (2002) Raising attainment of Pupils with Special Educational Needs. Interchange 67:5). Perhaps they prefer to wait to see if maturation will help. Or perhaps they are confused by the different terminology that is part of the dyspraxia scene and prefer to concentrate on helping the children no matter what their difficulties are called. Of course this decision is likely to depend on the age of the children, the level of difficulty they display and the expertise available to support them. Certainly children with the more severe difficulties should have a clinical assessment as soon as possible to ensure that the correct diagnosis is made.

It is interesting to find that many adults are coming forward for a formal assessment by a psychologist. This may be because, in comparing themselves to their friends, they have 'always known there was something making life different and difficult' (adult, age 33), and they wish to investigate the reason why. Naturally, they can be very resentful that their difficulties were not identified and supported much earlier for they may have been denied opportunities in higher education and/or in employment. Older children and students too need a formal diagnosis if they are to have accommodations made for their difficulties. These might be an IEP (individualised education plan) with a full movement component, the provision of a laptop to ease writing difficulties, special support on structuring their work or extra time for exams.

Clarifying the terminology

There is an ongoing and often heated debate over the terminology used to describe conditions very similar to dyspraxia. The first term is 'DCD (developmental co-ordination disorder)'. Some practitioners within the medical profession use this descriptor in preference to the term 'dyspraxia'. Asked to define the difference, they would claim that 'Children with DCD know what they want to do but have difficulty carrying it out, while children with dyspraxia have a praxis/planning problem and don't know what it is they wish to do' (Kirby & Drew, 2003). This could seem unnecessarily complex for practitioners in school.

Certainly DCD has been defined by a list of indicators in DSM-IV (See Appendix 1) while dyspraxia appears to hover as an amalgam of sensory integration, motor planning and motor execution difficulties with no specific cut-off point to determine who has or who does not have the condition. It is important to recognise that neither dyspraxia nor DCD is due to a general medical condition, e.g. cerebral palsy, neurological abnormalities such as tumour or global/pervasive developmental delay.

In America, Kaplan and her colleagues (2001) suggest that the term 'ABD (atypical brain development)' should replace 'dyspraxia'. This term indicates that children with a range of problems have a neurological difference that causes them to be less able in one aspect of their development. They suggest that all the conditions known in Britain as 'specific learning difficulties' could come under the ABD umbrella. In Scandinavia, children may be told they have DAMP, which is defined as disability in attention, movement and perception. There are those who prefer this term because it highlights the perception aspect of moving, just as Ayres (1972) did in her work on sensory integration.

In the past there have been other descriptors for dyspraxia too, e.g. 'the clumsy child', but this name was discarded because it seemed to apportion blame. It suggested that if the affected children were just to try harder, they would not be clumsy any more. This was patronising as well as being incorrect, for children with dyspraxia desperately want to be the same as their friends and they are very likely to be trying just as hard as they can.

Dyspraxia might well be called 'movement learning difficulties' in my view because that functional descriptor would give an immediate visual description of the condition. The first part 'movement' would pinpoint the area of difficulty and show exactly the kind of support that was required. The second part 'learning difficulties' would tell parents and teachers that these children were entitled to 'movement help'. Parents take it for granted that children with literacy or mathematical difficulties will have specialised and possibly individual teaching in school. Hopefully, an increased awareness of dyspraxia will lead to similar levels of assessment and support for movement difficulties. Only in that way can the maximum progress be assured. The name 'movement learning difficulties' could also be appropriate for other specific learning difficulties beyond dyspraxia where poor movement ability plays a significant part (see Figure 1.1).

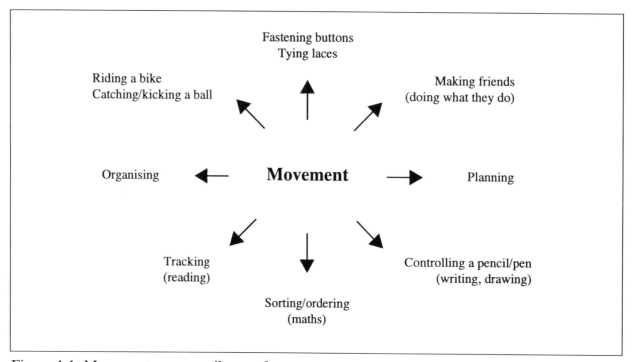

Figure 1.1: Movement as a contributory factor across a range of activities.

From this introduction it can be seen that the answer to the question 'what is dyspraxia?' is not straightforward at all. But as the preferred name within education is 'dyspraxia', this will be the one used in this book.

What effect does dyspraxia have?

Those who have dyspraxia find they have difficulty planning movements so that one action flows easily, rhythmically and almost effortlessly into the next. Most movements can be attempted but a great deal of practice is needed if they are to be done well. Some intricate movements can be impossible, especially if they happen at the midline of the body and necessitate two hands doing different things at the same time. Examples might be unscrewing a jar, winding a ball of wool or a yo-yo, slicing bread, opening letters, fastening buttons or wiping at the toilet. In these individual movements, timing is not usually a problem. However, many actions have to be done in a hurry, e.g. when others pressurise to have a turn, when a ball has to be passed to another player in a team or when a piece of work has to be completed in a specified time. Having to react quickly acts against careful planning and adds a great deal of stress to the day. Of course, having to rush may be because of a poor concept of time which some children and adults with dyspraxia have. For them 'ten minutes' may be a meaningless concept.

Many, even most, activities of daily living are affected by dyspraxia, just as most goals in education are. This is because at each stage the curriculum houses many practical activities.

Nursery	Primary	Secondary
Drawing	Sorting shapes at maths	Playing major games
Painting	Sequencing a story	Following instructions
Spreading at snack	Playing ball games	Following directions
Baking	Writing	Writing quickly
Early writing	Drawing	Ordering notes and resources
Getting clothes on and off	Reading maps	Reading maps
Toileting	Packing a school bag	Selecting books
Jigsaws and puzzles	Running and stopping	Knowing how much to learn
Cutting and pasting	Tessellation	Computing
Dressing dolls	Computing	Managing time

Figure 1.2: A sample of curriculum activities that depend on competent movement.

Teachers have to be sure that all children, but particularly those with dyspraxia, have the most appropriate equipment, e.g. left-handed scissors, lined paper for writing, instructions that are set out clearly in small steps/manageable stages, in fact everything that spells out good teaching. Then, because extraneous demands are reduced, the children can be 'freed up' to concentrate on the task at hand.

Discrepancy in intellectual and movement competence

Children affected by dyspraxia are of average or above average intelligence. While this is good news in that it means they can use their strengths to compensate for their area(s) of difficulty, it also means that they are able to self-evaluate. They know that they find some things more difficult than their peers do and as a result they often become overly critical of their own abilities. Parents and teachers telling them they are good at something when they know very well they are not, is not helpful at all; it is both patronising and demotivating. It is much better for helpers to be realistic, while at the same time setting out a positive plan for progress. In school several children can work together in activity groups, even although they might have slightly different targets in their IEPs. In this way they can build on their shared experiences and interests; they can practise and improve their skills together; and best of all perhaps, they can make friends – a real boost to their self-esteem.

Despite their intelligence, the descriptors that children and adults with dyspraxia often have to endure are 'awkward', 'clumsy', 'inept' and 'always last' and as these are both negative and hurtful, they are very likely to affect the self-esteem in a negative way. Although no one would deny that dyspraxia is debilitating, poor self-esteem can cause children to see themselves as having more profound disadvantages or more widespread difficulties than is actually the case and result in them feeling worthless, of little value to themselves or anyone else. Without early support, perhaps in showing them how to set realistic goals and supporting them as they are achieved, depression can set in. To prevent this, all the affected children, adolescents and adults need families and teachers who understand dyspraxia and the difficulties it brings. The best thing is for everyone who is concerned to build a trust relationship where they share experiences and strategies to help. This allows them to fully understand the effects of dyspraxia in the home and at school, for children may behave quite differently in the two environments. Many parents explain that they 'get the brunt of the children's frustration when they explode in the safety of their own home' and this can surprise teachers who have considered the same children to be too quiet and tried to stimulate them to be more expressive.

Question 2: How many people are affected?

The answer to this question, which is that around 6% of children have some degree of dyspraxia, surprises many teachers, for this means that there will be children affected by dyspraxia in every class (Keen, 2001). They are often less surprised to discover that boys feature more than girls in this number because, from their experience in their classrooms, they recognise that there are many more boys than girls presenting with each of the different specific learning difficulties. Kadesjo and Gillberg (1998) studying DCD in Finland reported a ratio 5.3:1. In Britain and Norway, a more usual claim is 4:1 (Portwood, 2000; Sovik & Maeland, 1986). When girls do have dyspraxia, however, they tend to be more severely affected (The Dyspraxia Foundation (2000) Praxis makes Perfect. Newsletter of the D.F.).

Questions as to why this should be so elicit no certain answers. Some researchers and teachers who have noted the same difficulties in siblings query the possibility of a genetic influence and indeed many parents will tell of family members 'who were always unco-ordinated'. And when they think back, they may realise with some consternation, that 'no one paid any attention'. The 'clumsy ones just got on with doing what they could, for no one understood' or perhaps onlookers did not know how to help. Others ask whether infections in the mother or in the newborn child cause the difficulties or whether oxygen deprivation during the birth process could be the culprit. Interestingly the medical literature denies this link, while much anecdotal evidence given by many mothers blames birth trauma as the cause. Teachers often query whether the fine motor skills more girls choose to use in their earliest years offset lurking difficulties by providing early practice; yet again there are nutritionists who claim that providing a dietary supplement can reduce difficulties. This would be an environmental effect although the individual's internal capacity to absorb the acids would play a part too. The cause poses a fascinating nature/nurture problem with no certain definitive answers as yet.

Question 3: What are the earliest signs?

In the early years especially, progress can be synonymous with the acquisition of movement skills. Parents – often very anxious ones – and health visitors monitor when each child achieves their motor milestones, e.g. when they can use a pincer grip, when they can sit unsupported, if and when they crawl, and when they eventually walk and talk. The norms of development (see Appendix 2) suggest there are times when specific skills should be gained and although children with dyspraxia learn to do most, they are achieved just within the 'normal' time span and at the lower end of competence.

Most parents want their children to be at least as far on as the child next door. The children themselves want to ride their bikes or tie their laces at the same time as their friends. When this does not happen, the whole family can be sorely perplexed by the children's inability to do things 'just as well and at the right time'. Moreover, these movement skills are the kinds of things children want to do. Unlike poor reading ability which can be hidden away, movement skills are public and peers can be cruel, quick to taunt and jeer. Often they refuse to let children with poor movement skills join in a game. Those who are affected by dyspraxia may resort to being the class clown or behaving badly to try to be accepted as part of a group. They may even withdraw from trying altogether.

Observing the children closely shows that a number of different factors may underlie the difficulties. These are discussed below.

Lack of strength

Some parents explain that 'from the earliest days, we knew there was something wrong.' This was because their babies had very poor muscle tone, i.e. hypotonia. Their children were floppy, and even after several days they were unable to support their heads and their limbs felt 'spongy, not firm and strong at all'. Often doctors reassured the parents, saying that they were overanxious, that they should give the baby time 'to strengthen up' and all would be well. This did little to comfort. When the children became able to move around, the differences, e.g. a strange gait due to a poor sense of balance, or poor co-ordination leading to the child dropping things, usually became more apparent and the parents' suspicions that there was something wrong were confirmed.

Hypotonia or poor muscle tone is found in many children with dyspraxia. If the top half of the body is affected, then fine motor skills such as writing and drawing, cutting and threading can be difficult and when the bottom half lacks strength, then the gross motor patterns of walking, running and combined actions such as running and jumping are frustratingly difficult. These movement patterns can be achieved, but at the lower end of a continuum of competence and usually just within the 'normal' time span.

Poor co-ordination

One of the earliest movement patterns, which depends on co-ordination, balance and timing, is crawling, a complex movement pattern requiring sequential movements of the limbs as weight-bearing changes. When parents suspect their child has 'something wrong' and bring them for assessment, they are often surprised to be asked if their child crawled and wonder what that has to do with the case. If they answer 'No', however, this provides just one pointer towards a diagnosis of dyspraxia. Nearly always, children who do not crawl, cannot crawl, i.e. they cannot manage the combination of co-ordination, balance and timing that would allow this to happen.

Often parents think that when their children move straight from sitting to standing with support to walking, they have missed a step, in other words that they have done well. Unfortunately, this is not always true. Not every child who does not crawl will have a specific learning difficulty, but many of them do. In Headstart (a special intervention programme to help literacy primarily for children who lack resources at home), and in perceptual-motor programmes, the activities always include crawling. This is because of the complex balance and co-ordination it requires. Sometimes parents and children are asked to crawl together and more than occasionally the adults are flummoxed to find they cannot do it either.

Sadly, those who never crawl miss more than the practice of just one movement pattern – which incidentally is the same one as used in climbing stairs on hands and knees – for in crawling the body is in a safe prone position. Even toppling over sideways causes no hurt, so lots of new combinations of movements can be safely tried. When a child stretches out to retrieve a toy or reaches up to get a drink, as just two examples, the movement requires a shift in weight-bearing from four points to three. If the outstretched arm wavers around as it does when stretching is new, constant small adjustments in balance have to be made. This provides a good rehearsal for when more sophisticated adjustments in balance are needed, e.g. in walking over rough ground or when carrying a heavy case or school bag. During the stretch the children are also learning about distance and direction, i.e. spatial concepts that tell how far away objects and people are. This is how they learn to perceive, i.e. to use all their senses together to guide their movements – a process called sensory integration (Ayres, 1972) or cross-modal transfer (Bee, 1999). As they perceive, they take in information from the environment, analyse it in the cerebral cortex of the brain and transfer that to the specific muscle that which initiate movement. Gradually, through practice, movements should become automatic/habitual, so that they do not require lots of pre-action planning. When they do not, the rate of processing is affected.

In dyspraxia this automaticity is often absent – it does not happen. This means that constant, conscious planning is required. Concentration with no automatic functioning results in those with dyspraxia having a very tiring day.

Poor body and spatial awareness

All movement is eased if children and adults have sound body and spatial awareness. Knowing where and how they are functioning in space makes their movements both effective and efficient. Placing a cup on a table needs recognition of where the hand is and the distance between the hand and the surface if the transition is to be safely made. Even drinking from a cup needs awareness of the tilt of the cup in relation to the position of the mouth. If the distance is misjudged, spills happen, clothes have to be changed and everyone gets cross.

These early practices are the foundations of later spatial decision-making, which could keep children safe, e.g. in timing stepping off the kerb while judging the distance of an oncoming car, or in the playground letting them know how far they can run before they crash into a wall. Children who have not had early experiences that have required practice of these basic movement abilities may find later movements that depend on them problematic.

Fortunately, there are many fun activities that can help. Games such as 'Simon says' (where, when instructed by the leader, the children 'put your hand on your elbow or your knee or your ankle') help children recognise their body parts and where they are in relation to one another. Singing games such as 'Head, shoulders, knees and toes' are enjoyable too. All the children can participate with no sense of 'picking' on the ones who have difficulty knowing where their body parts are. If body awareness is not well developed, then specially chosen activities to help should be part of a daily programme. (Suggestions are in Chapter 4.)

Poor planning and organisational skills

It is often difficult to recognise when very young children have planning and organising difficulties because so much tends to be done for them. However, there are clues, which could come from reflecting on the children's responses to events that occur in their day. When the family is getting ready to go out, do the children show signs of anticipating the trip – do they fetch their coats or get their shoes on without being reminded? Do they ask sequential questions about what will happen first then later on? Can they play contentedly without pining for adults to be involved? Do they play constructively, i.e. trying to make things and if they do, do they gather whatever they need or ask where these things can be found? Can they stay with an activity for a reasonable amount of time? Can they get their things ready for nursery or school or prepare for special happenings there? Do they think ahead and suggest what they would like in their lunch box? If they can do at least some of these things, this shows that they are thinking ahead and planning what comes next.

If planning, organising and sequencing appears to be problematic, encouraging the children to think ahead or to reflect can be done through a series of prompts, e.g. 'What shall we do after tea?' 'Can you check in the fridge to see what we'll need to buy for supper?' 'What could we have that is different from last night?' These sorts of interactions need to be thought through carefully. It is much simpler for parents just to do everything themselves, or rush on without bothering to recap the events of the day emphasising when they occurred, but these strategies are important in developing the short-term memory as well as helping planning and organising skills.

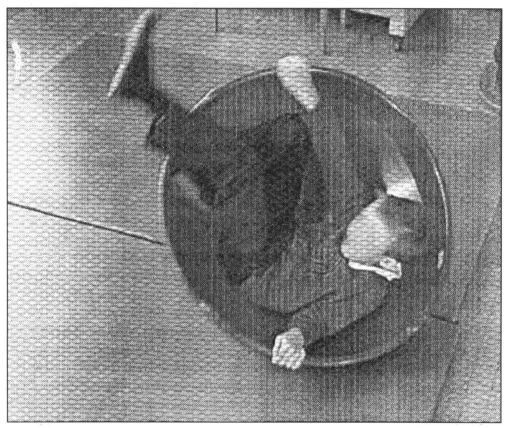

Greg enjoys the spinning top which helps awareness of his back because he must use (feel) his back to start the spin. He lacks awareness of where his feet are. They should be tucked into the top. If no support is given, all his gross motor skills may well be affected.

Poor short-term memory

One of the greatest frustrations for the child, their parents and their teachers is caused by the children's poor short-term or working memory. This causes them to forget how to do things they could do the day before. At 2 p.m. some children will not remember if they had lunch, far less be able to tell what they had to eat. Often these bright children will make up some kind of answer to disguise the fact that they do not know. Asked 'What did you do at school today?' they will answer 'nothing', possibly because they do not remember what went on. They are also likely to appear vague and unsure. This is different from the children who do not have the language to explain or who cannot take the time to tell because they have other more exciting things to do.

In the classroom and at home, patience often runs thin when explanations have to be given all over again. This is why routine is so important. Repetition fixes things in the short-term memory as do charts, timetables and lists but the most important thing is for everyone to realise that a poor short-term memory is part of the condition and that constant probing to find if the children are remembering is stressful. If this is overdone, the children are likely to switch off. With help in the form of patient reminders and subtle ways of asking for assistance, the children *will* remember. Additional strategies to help them do so should be part and parcel of any support package.

Question 4: Do people grow out of it?

Unfortunately, dyspraxia just does not go away. Maturation alone is not enough to resolve all the problems. Some would say that adolescents and adults can make choices about what they do and this lets them avoid the things they cannot. This sounds an ideal solution, but it is not straightforward at all, for 'avoiding things' still involves planning and organising how this is to be done, as well as selecting and organising the resources for the alternative activity.

So how do people with dyspraxia cope? Listen to Jack and Sian and find out how dyspraxia affects their day.

Firstly Jack who is eight and who has been put in the bottom language group despite having lots of good ideas for stories and being orally bright. His writing, however, is almost illegible.

Figure 1.3: Comparison of Jack's story writing by hand and on the computer.

Jack explains:

'I can see good writing in my head but it doesn't come out on paper anything like that. It's the worst you could see – all squiggles with the letters different sizes and sometimes on top of one another. I try to hold the paper steady but it wriggles away and gets all smudged. It makes me want to cry but boys don't, do they? When I asked my teacher, "what's wrong?" she shook her head and said we'd try lined paper and promised that would help. I couldn't manage that either, so I scrunched it up and put it in the bin. I don't write stories any more now except when I really have to. I just sit and dream.'

14

Jack had very low muscle tone in his shoulders and fingers so it was no surprise that he found controlling his pencil difficult. He also found that when his two hands had to do different things – one holding the paper while the other wrote – his difficulties increased. Eventually, after his parents pushed hard for a detailed diagnosis (which was dyspraxia and dyslexia), the school provided a laptop for some of the day. Now that his hands did not need to cross the midline of his body or be engaged in different kinds of actions at the same time, he was able to express his thoughts more fluently and he was able to have the credit his imaginative work deserved. An added bonus was that the other children envied him his acquisition.

Secondly Sian who is 12 and has just gone to secondary school. She tells how her poor planning and organisational skills let her down. She explains:

'I was really dreading going to a huge secondary school because in my primary, I knew where everything was and what to do on each day. We only had one teacher who took us most of the time and she was lovely. She knew I had dyspraxia and although she never made a fuss, she was always there checking up that I was managing and if something got lost or broken she wasn't cross. Sometimes I couldn't get my homework done because I had to go for exercises, but she understood how important they were – anyway I could do most of the important things like maths and that pleased her.'

'When I had to go to the secondary, everything was so confusing. All the first years had a "buddy" to show them around, but sometimes my one didn't turn up and I couldn't remember where to go for classes. When some of the other girls found out that I got lost easily they actually told me the wrong way to go – that really hurt – and they laughed when I got a row for being late. My dyspraxia is quite mild and I didn't want to let everyone know I was different from them, so Mum and I didn't tell the new school at the start, but we've had to now and it's much better.'

Question 5: Should children have a label?

Sian raises the important question of labelling. Many parents and teachers are unsure of the pros and cons of 'having a label' which results from a clinical diagnosis. Some are listed here:

- A diagnosis of dyspraxia means that the children have a recognised condition. The parents can be sure that the children are not just being tiresome or careless and that their parenting skills are not at fault. They can share this with the staff in school. This in itself can give some relief.
- Parents, teachers and other school personnel can then find out about and discuss dyspraxia, recognise that this is not the children's fault and plan strategies that can reduce their children's stress. Everyone can be assured that with the correct support, progress can be made. This will involve the children in a great deal of practice that other children do not have to do, but the effort can bring positive results. School professionals have to recognise that children with dyspraxia do have these extra, tiring activities and reduce other demands on their time and energy.
- Having a label can have negative connotations in that their peers see the children as different. This may act for them in that allowances are made for their difficulties, or against them if 'being different' is seen as unacceptable. The danger is that adults, understanding all the implications of dyspraxia, may ascribe difficulties that the children do not have, rather than looking at the individual profile of abilities as well as difficulties that each child presents.

- As there is no cut-off point to distinguish between those who have and those who do not have dyspraxia, those making the diagnosis may be reluctant 'not to give a label' in case they are mistaken and the children are denied specific help. In borderline cases they may play safe rather than say that there is no need for a label at all. Professionals are increasingly afraid of litigation. This may lead to over-labelling.
- A label is necessary if funding is to be sought. Allowances in terms of finance or resources can be available if the children need extra support.

Summary

What competencies do children need to move well? What kind of support could help?

- Confidence to try

This requires a positive self-concept/recognition of safety precautions/motivation to make the attempt.

Support: Someone to boost the children's self-esteem; who can analyse the demonstrated movement pattern, suggest the next stage and give warm praise for trying. Someone who, implicitly or explicitly, conveys the idea that success can be achieved.

- Knowing what to do: conceptualising the idea

This requires imagination/realism; previous experience/memory; a role model; recognition of possibilities and selection of appropriate ones.

Support: Someone who can suggest alternatives and build on tentative suggestions in a way that is appropriate and realistic in terms of the children being successful.

Planning, organising and sequencing

This requires the ability to think ahead; to order actions; to anticipate obstacles; to solve problems (e.g. recognising what strategies will be most likely to achieve goals or meet targets). Devising, remembering and keeping rules can also be important.

In movement terms, children need to get the body ready before, during and after movements, i.e. know which body parts to move at what time. They also need to know how to move sequentially.

Support: Someone who can analyse the transitions between movements. Someone who can analyse what they see as it happens to ascertain what is amiss.

Perceptual abilities

Perceptual acuity is needed for the child to take accurate sensory cues from the environment and use them together to guide movement. Accurate spatial decisions depend on perception. When the senses are used together to inform the mover, sensory integration results. (More detail in Chapter 3, Understanding sensory integration and the part the senses play in helping children learn and move).

Support: Someone who can determine the difficulty and intervene appropriately. This may mean providing resources or finding gradual ways of extending tolerance.

Movement abilities

These are required to enable children to move in a co-ordinated, balanced and rhythmical way, i.e. using the correct selection of strength, speed and space so that momentum makes the movement flow. Children should be able to cope with transitions and use feedback from a first attempt to improve the next try (see Chapter 4 Observing and assessing movement: knowing how to help).

Support: The children need someone who has the observational skills to find where the difficulty lies; who can analyse the basic movement patterns and work out the practices that are needed to develop skills. Some children may benefit from a demonstration as this provides a visual picture of what they are attempting to do.

Physical/neurological development

The children must have the neurological development and the physical wherewithal to make the movement possible. This means they must have developed adequate myelination of the axons within the brain to allow messages to transmit quickly and accurately. They also need the length of limb and body build that will allow the activity to be done (see Chapter 2 for details on myelination).

Support: The children need someone who can advise on the kinds of activities that would encourage myelination and co-ordination, e.g. crawling (Goddard, 2002) or suit the body build, e.g. non-contact sports such as table tennis for the more fragile children. Someone who will watch and support in a first/second/third try.

Memorising abilities

These are required if children are to be able to repeat previously learned movements; to use the feedback from one movement to help the next; to habituate movements so that they become automatic.

Support: The children need someone who can prompt recall imaginatively without using too many closed questions such as 'What did you do yesterday?' These suggest one-word answers. It is better for adults to make statements such as 'I remember being very pleased when you managed to (name the activity). Tell me how you managed to do that'. These positive interactions stimulate a much longer response.

Reflex inhibition

Being able to use the postural reflexes – having the primitive reflexes inhibited at the correct time. As just one example, Goddard (1996, 2002) explains that if the asymmetric tonic neck reflex is retained, the development of fine motor skills such as writing is likely to be delayed. She has developed a programme of exercises to reduce/eliminate the impact of 15 retained reflexes.

Support: Someone trained in the process of reflex inhibition.

Nutrition

Being able to absorb and utilise fatty acids to allow flexibility and adaptation.

Support: Parents, teachers and children need nutritional advice about taking fatty acids.

This chapter ends on a positive note for although there is no cure for dyspraxia and maturation alone does resolve the problem, with appropriate assessment, support and positive encouragement, children and adults *can* make considerable progress. More and more schools are implementing daily perceptual-motor programmes which are based on continuous assessment and considered support. Surely this is very good news?

Chapter 2
Understanding children's development and the impact of having dyspraxia

In an ideal world, every child from the moment of conception would have the best chance to be a happy, healthy individual. This would mean that both nature, i.e. the 'genetic blueprint which influences what we can do' (Bee, 1999), and nurture, i.e. the environmental factors which to some extent control these things, would work together to provide the maximum succour and support. Even then, however, the child who is at the centre of it all will interact with 'what he has inherited and where he is brought up' to make his own life chances.

But of course the world is not ideal and such a state of affairs does not always happen. Instead a myriad of factors, both positive and negative, impinge on the growing child. Even before birth, both genetic factors (i.e. the inherited pattern of genes) and environmental ones (e.g. the mother's age, level of stress, diet and lifestyle), influence the development of the foetus so that the newborn has an individual pattern of characteristics. Increasingly as confidence and competence grow, children will use their abilities and attributes to make a life contribution of their own.

Prenatal	Perinatal	Post-natal
Genetic influence? Many families have several members affected by dyspraxia	Ischaemia – poor oxygen supply to the baby?	Poor nutrition?
Mother's diet – inadequacy – affecting development?	Other birth traumas?	Delayed myelination of the axons?
Hormonal imbalance, e.g. thyroxin?	Caesarean where the baby does not take part in the birth process	
Alcoholism?		
Infections, e.g. rubella at a critical developmental stage, mumps, HIV?		

Figure 2.1: Some factors possibly influencing development.

The fact that children are all inherently different with environmental factors influencing even the unborn child makes the study of child development both fascinating and complex. How can one begin to understand development when no two children are exactly the same? This is just possible because all children follow a common pathway. Some move along it slowly and haltingly while others appear to run but there are recognisable steps and stages that all children pass through to reach their very different levels of attainment. Sometimes these blend so that the new skills are practised before the older ways are abandoned; sometimes they appear as sudden changes in thinking and growing. When children do this, i.e. when they 'suddenly' understand conservation or 'suddenly' shoot out of their clothes, they can surprise everyone, even those close to them. These changes are only loosely tied to chronological age, e.g. the 'normal' time for walking would be 12–18 months, but they do provide an indication of the kind of progress the children should be making at different ages. These are the norms of development (see Appendix 2), formed by studying large groups of children and averaging their attainment. Children with the specific learning difficulty dyspraxia will be progressing as a younger child in the perceptual-motor and very likely the social and emotional aspects of their development. Their intellectual component should not be affected.

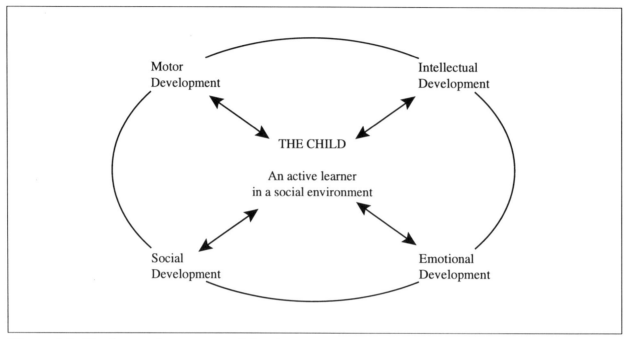

Figure 2.2: The interacting aspects of development.

While these separate aspects do have identifiable features, they are really separated out to make the study of development manageable. This is an artificial division because all the aspects interact. The child who has learned to crawl (physical and motor development), as just one example, can now explore the environment and so confront many problem-solving challenges, e.g. how can I empty this cupboard? These develop intellectual abilities and social ones too. Perhaps these latter ones are especially called upon when he or she is found out. On the other hand children faced with new uncertainties, e.g. going to the dentist or into hospital, may well regress and behave as they did at a younger age. Perhaps their toilet training is affected. They may even become reluctant to speak.

At times of stress most people revert to an earlier way of coping or not coping. This affects the assessment of the listed competencies. Think of the apparently socially confident child who cries and clings when going to nursery for the first time. Think of adults at interviews who find they are interacting in an inappropriate manner yet cannot stop; think of taking a driving test and finding that previously smooth changes of gear suddenly screech again. No matter how mature people are, their 'performance' can be severely affected by the stresses of the day. For most, this regression is temporary, for once the stress is removed then the abilities that seem to have been lost, return. The feelings of frustration and inadequacy, however, can be recalled. These mirror the effects of having dyspraxia.

Children with dyspraxia have a number of hurdles that other children do not have. Depending on the level of 'dys' ability, these set limitations on the rate of the children's progress. How well each one copes depends on many factors. The positive experiences and support they are given at home, at school, by their friends and by the wider community are some. The intrinsic level of perseverance and willingness to work much harder than others to gain success can influence achievement too. These are all tremendously important in boosting the children's self-esteem. The effect will also be determined by the extent dyspraxia impinges on the activities the children would like to be able to do. Obviously a football-mad child who is unable to kick a ball is likely to consider dyspraxia more of a handicap and resent having it, more than one who prefers reading and enjoys more sedentary hobbies. These skills are unimpaired unless a reading difficulty is co-occurring. In that case the child would have a dual diagnosis, i.e. dyspraxia and dyslexia.

This interchange across the different aspects of development makes it hard to place certain competencies accurately in the correct one. Consider 'communication'. Most people would see this as being part of social development. If this is spoken language, however, there is a huge intellectual contribution in understanding the words and knowing which words to use when. There is a social requirement in waiting for a turn and appreciating the kind of language and tone of voice that would be appropriate. Emotional competences are called upon when empathising with the speaker, while confidence and understanding is necessary to continue the conversation.

On the other hand if communication is non-verbal, i.e. made through gestures and facial expressions, then the physical/motor and emotional aspects of development are the most relevant places for 'communication' to be placed. The physical/motor contribution determines whether the voice apparatus in the mouth can be controlled and manipulated to allow words to be spoken clearly. Children who have verbal dyspraxia have specific and quite complex language difficulties and must be referred to a speech and language therapist without delay. They may have no other symptoms of dyspraxia at all, although most of the children have some co-ordination difficulties too.

The analysis of activities into distinctive aspects naturally leads to observation and assessment to see how well each of these things is done. To gain a complete picture, observations should be carefully recorded in different environments and if possible by different people so that they provide evidence of 'usual' ways of behaving/doing things. This evidence can form the basis of rich discussions among different professionals and so ensure that each child has the most comprehensive and accurate diagnosis.

Social and emotional development

Temperament

It is important, however, not to make assumptions as to how different children will cope, for this will be influenced by their temperament, i.e. 'the expression of the individual's emotional nature, regarded as dependent on constitutional make-up and therefore largely hereditary in origin' (Allport, 1937). Much later, Thomas and Chess (1977) still claim that temperamental characteristics are inherent in the child and see differences as 'reflections in the underlying variations in the ways a child's brain, nervous system or hormonal system operates'.

Other researchers, however, consider the influence of the child's context, e.g. the mother's child-rearing practices, as having a real influence on the children's temperament and so they consider temperament to be a dyadic characteristic (St James-Roberts & Wolke, 1994). Bee (1999) confirms the effects of temperament when she explains that sunny-natured resilient children find it easier to overcome the effects of disadvantage as they see the best of everything on offer. In the same situation, more vulnerable children tend to focus on the worst aspects and become depressed and/or less able to cope.

Why is it so important to understand temperament? When a specific learning difficulty is discovered the children's own reactions will, to some extent, determine how they will confront the idea and the implications of having it. Whether and to what extent this can be modified/exacerbated by those around them and how this can best be done are critically important questions for the children themselves and for those who seek to support them. Bates (1989) claims that 'if a child has supporting and loving parents who are able to deal with the child's difficulties, the child does not develop broader social problems.' But if the parents show that they are disappointed in their child, or lack child-rearing skills or have other stresses which prevent them giving adequate support, then the vulnerable child with difficulties is likely to have serious problems relating to others, i.e. in making and keeping friends. Such claims could be the source of even tremendously supportive parents feeling 'guilty' that they have failed their child in some way. Sometimes despairing parents will share their bewilderment, saying 'maybe there's a right way of doing things that I don't know about – maybe I don't do the right things.' They can become overwhelmed by the realisation that the individuality of each child in a different context can mean that strategies that help one child have to be tried and amended to suit another. It is not straightforward to be a parent at all.

Understanding friendships

Children with dyspraxia very often find difficulty in making and retaining friends. To try to understand the process, researchers have observed children in groups at play and watched to see how friendships were formed. In these studies children who were consistently positive and supportive were the ones who were chosen as leaders or friends (Black, 1992). They also found that children who were consistently aggressive were often rejected.

Popular children	Rejected children
Friendly towards all other children	Not dependable
Extroverts, willing to share ideas	Sulky for some of the time
Physically attractive	Will not join in
Mature for their age	Cannot do things
Good at popular activities, e.g. ball games	Physically or verbally aggressive
Reasonably good at school	Tell tales

Figure 2.3: Characteristics of popular and rejected children.

Sometimes children with dyspraxia resort to aggression as an expression of their frustration at not being able to do so many movement activities that can be the basis of 'getting to play'. These impair progress in the classroom too. The other children are usually quick to spot these difficulties, sometimes with glee. A ten-year-old explaining his frustration with a piece of poor writing explained, 'I can see what I want to do in my head but it doesn't come out like that, no matter how I try.' This could be a typical response from a child with poor fine motor control. On the other hand, less articulate children might withdraw and give up trying altogether. They can then be blamed for 'not trying' and even be called lazy or uncooperative when this is far from the truth. The kind of response children make will, to some extent, depend on their temperament. Parents and teachers have to recognise the things the children can do well and give them every opportunity to respond in these ways.

While these researchers were considering temperamental traits, Macintyre and Deponio (2003) considered the underlying skills that were co-occurrent in specific learning difficulties. Perhaps lack of skill in specific areas prevented the children doing what their friends did, e.g. riding a bicycle or playing football, and this caused them to be left out of activities? Certainly many children with movement difficulties would claim that this is the cause. It is not difficult to see how their opportunities for social interaction are reduced by their lack of movement skills.

Case study 2.1

'I hate it when the football season starts,' explained Gordon who had dyspraxia, 'for I know I'll not get chosen to be in the game. Last year they said I could be a goalpost, but I got frozen and it was so boring. But I had to pretend it was good fun or I would have been left out altogether. This year the teacher said I was to be team manager, so when the others are playing she helps me to arrange things on the computer – we've invited another school to a match so there's plenty of work to do.'

Gordon's parents who had despaired were so pleased, especially when the teacher told the teams that the event had been organised by their son. So there are meaningful alternatives that can compensate – it takes time and imagination to think them up, but the children's increase in confidence very often helps them tolerate their other difficulties.

A different reason for being left out could be the difficulty many children with dyspraxia have in following rules. If this is the case they cannot anticipate changes in play or games and so they may inadvertently do the wrong thing, spoil the game and not understand why others jeer or scorn or say they cannot play any more. To try to compensate, the children can be helped to learn the rules or the routines. This can help, but if these change as the activity goes on, or if 'play rules' cannot be rehearsed in advance because no one knows how the play will develop, then the children who cannot understand or tolerate change are lost. How does one explain?

Rather like understanding rules, a more subtle problem some children with dyspraxia have is empathising with the unhappiness or pain of others. This involves projecting emotional understanding on happenings 'out there' rather than on something where the child is personally involved. This criterion does not occur in the DCM criteria for DCD and so may come from a co-occurrent or overlapping difficulty, perhaps a trace of Asperger's syndrome? Not appreciating the other person's hurt can result in them making inappropriate comments or not showing any sympathy, i.e. not empathising with the situation. This apparent lack of concern can lead to them being isolated, even rejected and they do not understand why.

For whatever reason, e.g. poor social, motor or emotional skills, many children with dyspraxia lack friends and can be baffled and hurt by not being accepted. They may even be bullied. To try to compensate, they may resort to aggressive behaviour or withdraw from the scene, asserting that they 'don't care!' Unfortunately, these very understandable strategies lead to rejection and adolescents especially may find that the only ones who will have them in a group are those who themselves have been rejected (Bee, 1999). Very often any friend is better than having no friend.

Boosting self-esteem

It is important for children to feel that others like them, for this kind of positive self-evaluation leads to a high self-esteem. Harter (1990) argues that the level of self-esteem children have, depends on two judgements. These are:

- the discrepancy between what the children think they would like to be and their own self-evaluations.
- the level of support they consider they have from people who are important to them.

In this respect, it is unfortunate that in the primary years children change from regarding their parents and teachers as the most significant people in their lives to valuing the opinion of their peers, because these may be less understanding and supportive. To keep the children's self-esteem high, these have to be positive. If not, parents and teachers have to find strategies to help. It is best if these are based on activities the children with dyspraxia like to do. Finding children with the same interests can help, as then the talk will be based on mutual understandings. If they are based on 'closed skills' such as fishing or finding out about dinosaurs or dressing dolls, the 'rules' do not change and so unexpected occurrences do not mar the pattern of events. Another helpful strategy can be inviting younger children to play. They will not be so advanced socially; they may well defer to the older child's ideas and so may fit well with the social developmental level of the dyspraxic child. In some areas there are friendship groups for children with specific learning difficulties and some children enjoy meeting youngsters with the same kinds of problems as themselves. At the very least they discover that they are not alone. Hopefully they will make a friend and then at school they can talk about their 'other friend', which can give their confidence a real boost.

All children, but particularly those with dyspraxia who are usually vulnerable children, have to be helped to focus on their strengths. Sadly, these may not be the traits the children themselves value. The question 'to what extent can support from others compensate for lack of skill?' is tantalisingly difficult. The most obvious strategy for them to adopt would be 'to be positive, to give lots of praise' and indeed this is a good thing to do, provided the donor tempers the input according to the responses of the children. These are likely to vary according to their age and the reactions of the peer group. If they are seen to be having too much attention without meriting it, then resentment could build up, making their day much worse. The worst scenario is when other parents add their comments without understanding the difficulties children with dyspraxia face.

When children are sad and have few friends, parents may try to compensate by giving treats in the form of sweets and crisps. If this is combined by lack of exercise because the children prefer to avoid sports, then the weight can pile on. Body image is a very important part of self-esteem, so it is important that children feel that they look good. Being overweight adds to negativity through 'being different' and gives the bullies another target to deride. Parents could perhaps investigate 'novel' activities which their children might enjoy, e.g. family jogging or hill or fell walking or fun swimming. These do not involve competition yet can be so rewarding in terms of health through developing strength and mobility and cardiovascular fitness. Just as important, the activities can assist the myelination of the neurones and axons, thus stimulating neurological development and helping the children's movement efficiency. In addition, the children can learn all about the activity in its environment and have some special news to report back to their classmates. But how do children develop the skills that allow them to participate in activities?

Physical development

Physical development underpins motor development because the growth pattern, e.g. the length of trunk and limbs, develops in partnership with strength and control. Sometimes one appears to overtake the other, e.g. when adolescents in the midst of a growth spurt seem unable to control their feet, but generally these work together to ensure that movement can be effective and efficient. This allows the children to do what they want to do without extraneous movements which would be both tiring and clumsy.

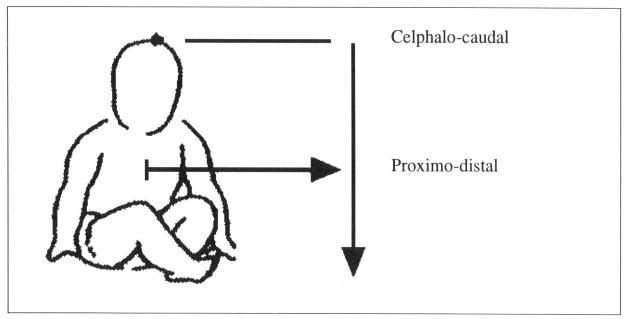

Figure 2.4: The process of physical development.

This developmental process is cephalo-caudal and proximo-distal. This means that babies control their heads before their backs are strong enough to allow them to sit and universally babies sit before they stand. All children stand before they walk and walk before they run. Control also begins at the trunk and takes time to reach the periphery (fingers and toes). This explains why grasping can be wavering and unsure for quite a time before the pincer grip is developed. Finding whether babies use their pincer grip is one of the early assessments of development health professionals make. The skill of 'letting go' is much harder to achieve. Objects tend to drop from babies' hands rather than be released with conscious control.

Hormones that are the secretions of the endocrine glands control growth at all ages, including pubertal growth and the physical changes of adolescence. The pituitary gland is often known as 'the leader of the endocrine orchestra' because it triggers the release of hormones from the other glands. The thyroid would not secrete thyroxine without this stimulus and as this is necessary for brain development prenatally, the importance of the duo cannot be overemphasised. Secretions from the testes and ovaries remain at a very low ebb until age seven or eight. Then andrenal androxin begins to be secreted and heralds the first changes of puberty.

Some key points about physical development

- These virtually universal patterns of development are influenced by maturation, i.e. the 'sequential unfolding of physical characteristics governed by instructions contained in the genetic code' (Bee, 2000). Thus heredity is particularly influential. But adequate nutrition

25

and sleep play a part too, as do experience and guided practice. Nature and nurture are working together to determine progress. Gender should also be considered, for at birth, although there are no major differences, girls are slightly ahead in some aspects of physical maturity and boys slightly more vulnerable, featuring more in infant mortality rates.

- Sufficient practice of movement skills is needed to maintain the physiological system. Practice above and beyond that, however, does not normally 'speed things up'.

This means that without intervention, children cannot be persuaded to walk or learn to kick a ball, i.e. to hurry their motor skill achievement, until the underlying maturational competencies are in place. Researchers who have aimed to disprove this have stimulated the babies' walking responses each day for several weeks (Tanner, 1990) and found that the early muscle power the babies developed meant that they could walk a month or so earlier than the control group who were left to develop naturally. While no one would suggest trying to do this for all babies – who walk anyway – it does show that early intervention in the form of specific practices done at least on a daily basis can be effective in promoting physical skill.

This being so, the amount of interaction with those more skilled can be seen to be very important. For even although very young children may not be able to 'move properly' in terms of physically responding, they may be watching and internalising movement patterns demonstrated by adults or other children and these may facilitate the children's earliest tries. They may store patterns in the memory for later use, building a repertoire of possibilities to try when their strength and balance and kinaesthetic awareness develop. When they do and when they have the physical skills to play, they are learning about sharing as well as developing skilled movement.

Certainly this would seem to be the case in learning language. Most adults immediately 'converse' whenever they come into contact with a baby. When they do they adopt a higher pitch and use simple language (motherese). This contributes markedly to the children's early development of language. If the children hold gaze and offer some response such as smiling, or at a year old making conversational sounds (monosyllabic babbling) to respond, the interaction is likely to be extended. When this happens the adult is likely to recast sentences, e.g. 'Where is your Teddy? I see Teddy over there. Would you like to have Teddy?' The child does not reply verbally, but is storing these repetitions as a basis for more elaborate language later on. The basis of language, i.e. turn-taking, is also being established. Could the same internalisation happen with motor development? Would very early demonstrations have the same advantage? Would passive movements, i.e. where the parent or therapist moves the children's limbs for them, help the movement pattern to be established? Would this really increase strength in 'floppy babies'? There are many important issues still to be explored. Are there examples from other cultures that would provide some data?

Ethnic differences in motor development

Afro-Caribbean children develop a little faster, both before and after birth, and walk earlier than other children. They have heavier bones and longer limbs and more musculature providing the wherewithal to so do. Asian children fall slightly behind these norms. Freedman (1979) investigating the differences suggested that the baby's level of activity or placidity could explain these. Kagan et al. (1994) replicated these studies in a comparison of Chinese, Irish and Euro-American newborns. They found that the Chinese babies were 'significantly less vocal, less irritable and less active' than those in the other groups while the Euro-American children showed the strongest reactions to sensory input, e.g. touch, smells and sights.

The conclusions were that as these were newborn babies, the differences could not be down to systematic shaping by the parents. Yet the immediate patterns of interaction were different. Chinese mothers talked much less to their infants (Kagan et al., 1994). As this was soon after birth, the interaction was not 'controlled' by the child being quiet. The important conclusion was that the similarity between the mother and the child's quieter temperament would strengthen this trait, thus exacerbating the cultural differences over time.

The importance of practice

Regular practice can make an enormous difference to the acquisition of skill. The tasks have to be broken down until each step is achieved and gradually built up to the full skill. It is important to remember that children need the holistic picture of what they are aiming for as well as the stage by stage preparation. Children very often surprise by what they can achieve if those who offer support recognise how hard it is and if they can have some success that encourages them to keep trying.

Questions as to whether there is a neurological difference and what these differences might be are at the forefront of research at this moment in time (Stein, 2001; Kaplan, 2001).

Neurological development

A full explanation of the development of the brain is beyond the scope of this text but some notes, which concern the development of movement, should be useful to those wishing to understand dyspraxia.

Changes in the nervous system are extremely rapid in the first two years. At birth, the brain stem, found at the top of the spinal column (and containing the pons and the medulla oblongata) and the midbrain are the most completely developed parts of the brain. These are in the lower part of the skull and are connected to the spinal cord. They regulate the basic competencies of sleeping, waking and elimination, attention and habituation and movements of the head and neck, i.e. basic survival skills. The brain stem contains all the nerves that carry messages from the body to the brain. It is where all the nerve pathways cross to the other side. It is so important that injury to the brain stem can result in death.

The basal ganglia, thalamus and hypothalamus and then the cerebellum work together. They are responsible for the organisation of the sensory, motor and autonomic systems. All the incoming sensory information travels through the thalamus to the specific area in the cortex and so it plays a vital part in sensory interpretation.

The basal ganglia organise movements and help ones that have required conscious control and concentrated practice to become automatic. Motor skills such as swimming, driving a car and tying laces are examples of this. Children with dyspraxia seem to lack this facility, as automaticity can be extremely hard, even impossible to achieve. The hypothalamus controls the hormones involved in regulating temperature, hunger and sexual behaviour. These then pass to the pituitary gland where they are stored or dispersed. The hypothalamus and pituitary gland form the limbic system that stimulates feelings.

The cerebellum, often known as the 'little brain', has two hemispheres which co-ordinate information received from the senses and so contributes to the body being balanced, co-ordinated and controlled. It also determines muscle tone which is vitally important in being able to produce precise movements.

The part less well developed at birth is the cerebral cortex, i.e. the mass of grey matter which surrounds the midbrain and is responsible for perception, movement, language and more complex thinking, e.g. imagining or problem-solving (Goddard, 1996). It has two hemispheres linked by the corpus callosum, a tract of millions of nerve fibres which can produce instant reaction and feedback, thus facilitating communication between the two hemispheres.

The corpus callosum is larger in females than males and may be more resistant to damage (Kirby and Drew, 2003), perhaps explaining why there are more boys than girls presenting with specific learning difficulties. Some tasks involve both hemispheres but each houses areas where vital skills are sited. Their execution, however, depends on both hemispheres. The messages pass from one to the other through the corpus callosum.

Hemispheric lateralisation

Although the two hemispheres look the same, they are organised to be responsible for different tasks. The left hemisphere, which controls sensory input from and movement of the right side of the body, is more involved in processing language while the other, i.e. the right hemisphere, controls emotion and spatial information. The right side uses visual or auditory information, the left side words. The right side would recognise someone's face but would not be able to say who it was. This specialisation continues through the pre-school years.

If there is any malfunction in this area of the brain then movement and language may both be affected. This may partially explain the co-occurrent difficulties in dyspraxia and dyslexia.

All of these components are composed of neurones and glial cells, which are present at birth. Thereafter the developmental activity within the brain concerns the development of synapses. This means a huge level of active growth for all parts of the neurone including the axons, i.e. the strands that carry the messages to the synapses. All of these branch to form dendrites and as they proliferate, they form a dense conglomeration called the 'dendritic arbor'. This proliferation happens in the first two years and causes the brain to triple in weight. This process is not even for there is an initial burst of synapse formation in the first year or so after birth followed by a 'pruning of synapses' in each area of the brain – a that which 'cleans up the wiring diagram' (Hutenlocher & Burke, 1994).

An example may help to explain. A baby stretching to grasp a toy will 'waver and hover' around the object before grasping it. However, with maturation and practice, the action becomes increasingly accurate and dextrous. What is happening is that the most useful pathway in the brain is being reinforced, so that when this action is required again, it is precise and no fumbling is necessary. The extraneous pathways which are not needed are washed out so that they do not confuse later attempts.

This process is called 'dendritic pruning'. Bertenthal and Campos (1994) claim that 'experience does not create tracings on a blank tablet; rather experience erases some of them'. This pruning does not happen in all parts of the brain at the same time. Pruning in the part that has to do with vision happens around four months of age while the pruning in the language comprehension and production areas happens at about three years of age. Pruning continues through childhood and adolescence. This means that synaptic density in childhood is greater than in adulthood.

To begin with, the activity of nerve cells is stimulated by activity intrinsic to the brain, but it is the 'timing and patterning of external stimulation which determines the precise detail of neural networks – i.e. through editing, sorting and pruning connections' (Meadows, 1993). This process is the basis of the intellectual development that allows children to make sense of the experiences they have.

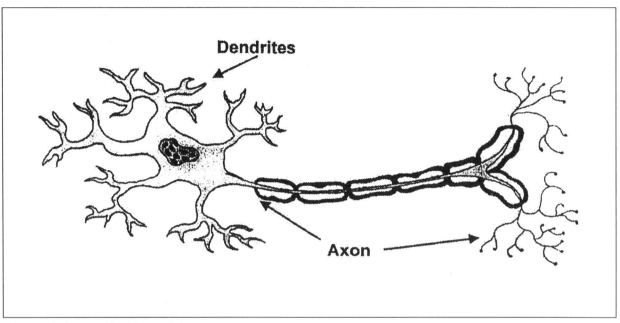

Figure 2.5: Myelination of the axons.

Myelination of the axons is another important development in producing dexterity. Myelin is a protective substance which coats the axons just like insulating tape. This ensures that the messages within the brain travel directly on the most efficient and direct pathway rather than sparking off to contaminate other messages. Myelin improves the conductivity of the nerves and allows responses to be accurate and quick, contributing to more streamlined cognition.

When multiple sclerosis occurs, the myelin breaks down – a reversal of the early process. This means that the competencies in the part of the brain that has been affected will become increasingly less controlled. Movements become clumsy, needing a greater amount of conscious control. Automaticity disappears and in time the ability to move without support may be lost.

NB The parts of the brain that govern movement are not fully myelinated until age six (Todd et al., 1995).

This finding is very important in considering dyspraxia and the other specific learning difficulties where poor movement competence makes a significant impact on progress. It also explains why teachers and parents are anxious to 'wait and see', hoping that with maturation and support the children will be able to catch up. Beyond age six, however, specialist assessment and intervention is likely to be required.

Hand dominance: confused laterality

Hand/foot preference or dominance is an interesting concept. While most three-year-olds will use either hand or foot without showing preference, by age six, dominance should be established. Heredity plays a part as dominance patterns run in families; 85–90% of the population would describe themselves as right-handed as they use that hand first in tasks such as eating, holding a pencil or throwing a ball, while 8–10% would say they were left-handed and 3% would claim to be ambidextrous.

29

For right-handed people, the left side of the brain controls movement and language while the reverse is true for those who are left-handed. An important question asks, does this matter?

Left-handedness

Left-handed people appear to have less strong hemispheric domination, enabling them to use either hand or foot with greater ease than their right-handed friends. This means:

- that they are likely to be better at tasks that require spatial skills, e.g. architecture or mathematics;
- that should the brain be injured, the other side of the brain can take over some of the tasks which it would not usually control.

Some interesting 'disadvantages' in being left-handed are apparent too.

Left-handers are over-represented in the numbers of children with specific learning difficulties, allergies, migraines and speech impediments such as stuttering. Of course, this does not mean that all left-handed children will have one or more of these disadvantages. It means that there are more left-handed children in the groups who do. More boys than girls are left-handed too.

Reflex inhibition

Of particular interest is the current work on reflex inhibition at the Institute for Neuro-physiological Psychology (INPP) in Chester. There, practitioners under the guidance of Peter Blythe and Sally Goddard have developed a non-invasive approach to helping children with learning difficulties. They 'check to see if the child can voluntarily direct his responses or if he is still governed by primitive patterns of response' (Goddard, 2002). If the children show that they have retained any of the primitive reflexes (automatic stereotyped movements directed by the brain stem and without involving the cortex), a programme of exercises specifically designed to reduce/eliminate these is given. The aim is for postural reflexes to take the place of the primitive ones, for these allow the children to be enabled to respond in a more mature way.

There are 15 such reflexes to be considered. All the work is relevant to children with dyspraxia but only one example can be given here. This is the ATNR (asymmetrical tonic neck reflex). In babies, if the head is turned to the side, the arm and leg on that side will extend while the other side will flex. Holt (1991) explains that as this reflex is present at the time babies are first seeing an object and reaching out to grasp it, 'the nervous system is making sure that the appropriate arm is stretching out towards the visualised objects.' This reflex should be inhibited by six months of age so that more mature movement patterns can develop. If not, if the primitive ATNR is retained, the cross-crawling pattern cannot happen and balance may be insecure due to the limb straightening response upsetting the centre of balance.

If children with dyspraxia have retained these reflexes and if the exercises can work to overtake them, then practice should ease their difficulties and allow their real intelligence to shine through.

Intellectual development

The question of what intelligence is, i.e. what aspects of behaviour can be called 'intelligent', is a very important one. In the past IQ scores were used as predictors of academic success. Children with dyspraxia would have a higher score on a traditional IQ test (which was only designed to measure the specific range of skills needed for success in schools) than if practical competences were measured. Such findings, i.e. that there were other important differences in children, prompted researchers to consider a wider range of attributes as meaningful indicators of success in life. Gardner (1983) suggested six kinds of intelligence: linguistic, musical, logical-mathematical, spatial, bodily kinaesthetic and personal. Children with dyspraxia would be likely to have most difficulty with the spatial and bodily kinaesthetic kind.

Then Sternberg (1986) claimed that intelligence could be subdivided into three parts, i.e. he offered a triachic theory of intelligence. The first part he named 'componential intelligence', which mirrors the kind of competences measured by an IQ test. Being able to plan and organise, to remember facts and apply them in new situations were the skills envisaged under this heading. The second he called 'experiential intelligence'. Someone with this is creative, able to make new connections and imagine new outcomes. The third part of the trio is 'contextual intelligence'. Sternberg identified those who had this kind of intelligence 'street smarts', i.e. people who were able to adapt their behaviour to suit different contexts whenever they judged that so doing would be to their advantage. In Britain they might be called 'street wise'.

All of these types of intelligence are umbrella terms for the skills children need to flourish in their lives. Wood (1994) provides a helpful list of competences which teachers should strive to develop in their children. These are:

- a desire and ability to attend, concentrate and memorise;
- knowing how to apportion one's time and resources in order to study and learn;
- possessing the confidence and expertise to present and explain oneself;
- knowing how to make what one has to write or say accessible to one's audience;
- the ability to evaluate and redirect one's efforts, to self-direct and self-instruct;
- knowing how to make one's attentions and actions contingent upon the requests, demands and needs of others.

He attests that difficulties in these areas will leave the child with problems. It would seem that the inability to remember could be at the root of them all.

Understanding memory: dependence on routine

Children with dyspraxia can become very frustrated by the effects of having a poor short-term memory. Remembering can be achieved but a great deal of rehearsal and 'extra' practice is needed to mitigate its effects. The children find it extremely hard to retain new learning, even for a short spell of time. Those who find concentrating and/or paying attention difficult find the problem is made worse. To try to overcome the effects of these 'dys' abilities, many of the children establish a routine. This gives them security in that they can anticipate what comes next and so they have time to prepare acceptable responses. It does mean, however, that they are less flexible in their approach. Furthermore, any deviance from this routine can make them extremely upset. Sometimes change can cause the children to be so excitable that they fail to listen to the instructions they are given. Then they find solving problems or following directions beyond them. Yet they are intellectually quite capable of solving them. The strategy rather than the intellectual demand lets them down.

Many children with dyspraxia know that spontaneity is not one of their strengths. When this is required they can feel inadequate because they know they may interact inappropriately. This can be caused through not quite grasping the tenor of a conversation in time or not empathising with the other person in the duo. Poor memory may well affect this, as remembering previous interactions and how they were carried out may need more time than is available, if they can be recalled at all. Misreading non-verbal cues may also be a significant deterrent to 'joining in'. As these carry 90% of the message in any interaction (Argyle, 1969), meeting new people with new or different patterns of behaviour and conversation can be overwhelmingly difficult. This has to be considered by teachers when they organise their children to learn/co-operate/discuss in groups.

What, then, is involved in remembering?

To understand memorising or remembering, it is useful to make a distinction between sensory store, short-term memory and long-term memory (Meadows, 1993). Sometimes the short-term memory is called 'the working memory'.

A huge amount of information from the environment comes in through the senses (see Chapter 3) to the short-term memory store. The capacity of this store is limited, however, and much of this information is lost or consciously discarded. The processes of selection, attention and concentration, however, result in the most personally valued information being retained in the short-term memory. This again is limited in size and so much information does not pass to the long-term store.

At each stage, control mechanisms help information to be retained. Practices like rehearsal help items to pass into the short-term memory.

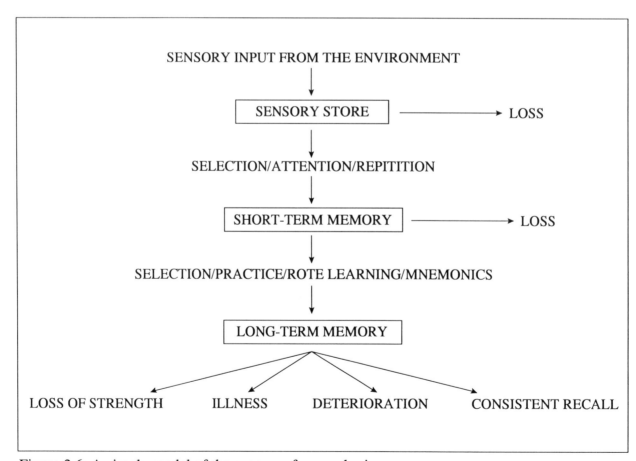

Figure 2.6: A simple model of the process of remembering.

32

Rehearsal

This is simply repeating items that have to be remembered many times, e.g. in memorising a telephone number until it can be written down or 'rules' such as 'i' before 'e' except after 'c'. Many children will do this automatically while others need to be shown how. This is similar to rote learning, which helps recall to become automatic and quick. Mind maps (Buzan, 1993) are particularly valuable memory aids for those who learn best visually. Instead of trying to remember all the items to pack in a school bag, a visual picture of 'things for my project', that is a global picture which can then be broken down, stimulates recall much more easily.

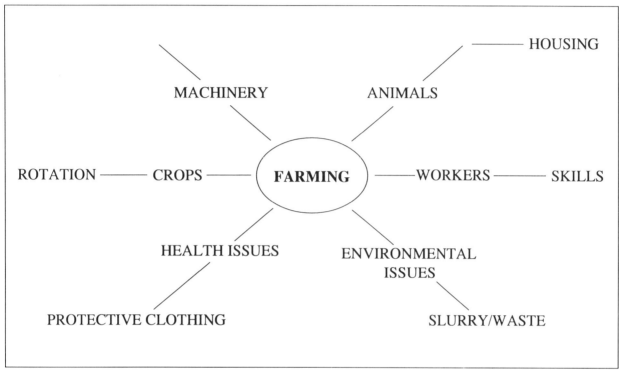

Figure 2.7: A mind map for a school project.

Mnemonics also help items to be retained in the long-term store. They may remain there for years, although sometimes the method can be retained without the meaning – as in learning times tables without really understanding why the answers are as they are. They are useful in exams as coping with one 'leading letter' at a time can give a structure to an answer. This could be a particularly useful aid for children who become stressed fearing that their memory will let them down. Many questions need to be confronted about examinations which, in my view, often measure endurance and memory before the knowledge and understanding that should be the critical content. Howe (1989), however, claims that retrieval processes like these can be problematic for children with specific learning difficulties. The strategies need to be explained and illustrations that are meaningful to the child used as exemplars.

There are environmental influences beyond the intellectual ones which impinge on the memorising process, e.g. personal preferences as to what is important, aims and goals advised by others; cultural influences and the level of knowledge/understanding/imagination to visualise what should be retained.

It is evident that the number of cognitive processes and strategies people have, increase with age and experience. Older people usually know more and do more things. Through role modelling and explanations, and trial and error experiences, teachers are able to suggest alternative ways of doing things. They also try to match their input to the preferred way of learning of each pupil so that memorising can be facilitated. The space or capacity of each memory store increases with development (growth and maturation) too, so that there is the possibility of more information being retained. It is important to note, however, that the size of the store is less important than the size of the space that can be used for more complex operations such as problem-solving.

Case (1985) suggests that children 'have general regulatory processes which regulate their mental activity'. He describes these as:

- a tendency to problem-solving;
- a tendency to exploration;
- a tendency to imitation;
- a capacity for mutual regulation with other people.

Problem-solving involves children searching their memories for a strategy which will answer a question or make a change/improvement or adapt something to fit a new situation. As children with dyspraxia have difficulty with recall, this can be problematic for them if they have not retained experiences for comparison.

In exploration the children try out various ways of extending their learning. A requisite is 'knowing what to do' and some children with dyspraxia find this difficult as well. They often resort to imitating others rather than conceptualising plans. This can give them a sort of success but can lead to resentment (by the model) or confusion if the model does not make the correct response.

Imitation leading to learning is much more complex than at first it would appear. Those who are copied need to explain clearly the whys and wherefores of their actions. Especially with an expert or practised model, much of what they do is done without conscious planning, so those demonstrating may fail to understand why copying is not straightforward. In addition, there may be skills that the copier is unable to do. Student teachers learning from experienced teachers experience such difficulties. This is because the skills that experienced teachers have are built up gradually and depend to some extent on the relationships with the children in their class. When the student teacher attempts to copy their overt behaviour, the subtleties are lost, the relationship is different, the student's non-verbals do not give the same messages to the children and so the outcome does not mirror the teacher's success.

The last of the four strategies cited by Case is having 'a capacity for mutual regulation with other people'. By this he means a child being able to adapt to another person's feelings, i.e. empathising and acting appropriately. This would involve reading non-verbal behaviour and interpreting the nuances of conversations. For those who take phrases literally, e.g. 'Watch your step,' or who find it impossible to read expressions that carry meaning, this would be hard indeed.

If children with dyspraxia have difficulties using these strategies, can they be helped to learn them? It appears that memory strategies such as rehearsal and categorisation can readily be taught to children without specific learning difficulties as young as age six or seven (Lange & Pierce, 1992). Widening the experience of children who have them, while at the same time reinforcing 'useful things to remember', is helpful in letting the children appreciate and remember the key features within a situation (Macintyre & Deponio, 2003). Linked to opportunities for reflection and recall, this could be the first stage in metacognition or helping the children recognise how they learn.

Metacognition

If children develop a range of strategies to solve problems and are helped to be aware of what they are doing when, the hope is that they will transfer these, i.e. use them again in appropriate situations and recognise the efficacy of doing so. This does not come easily to children with dyspraxia because they do not readily habituate, i.e. see the similarities in different situations and use already-practised actions again. They have to learn everything as a first time try and so they can be exhausted by the end of the school day. When the children are asked to practise things at home that are likely to spell more failure, it is not surprising that the suggestion is usually met with refusal or resentment. A complete change of activity where the children are likely to experience success is more likely to refresh the children and help boost their confidence. Then hopefully the necessary practices can be tolerated with more equanimity.

Metamemory

As the children learn about the most effective ways to tackle problems, Meadows (1993) advises that they should also be helped to recognise how they used their memories. This understanding she calls 'metamemory'. They could reflect, perhaps, on whether they remembered to use the mind map they had prepared and evaluate to what extent this strategy had helped. This reflection would help to build expert knowledge.

Building expert knowledge

This is where parents can really help. If they could discuss forward planning with the teacher and find the theme for the coming weeks, they could ensure that the children's background knowledge would be such that they would be able to make a contribution in class. This is not pre-teaching the main skills of the lesson but rather helping the children understand the context of what they were about to learn. A visit to a farm for the young ones or to an observatory or castle for the older ones – any kind of linked visit or experience – would help, especially if careful explanations were made. These could help the child make a useful contribution in class and so win genuine praise from the teacher and the other children.

Cognitive styles

Over the years there have been attempts to identify cognitive styles or preferred ways of learning. The ultimate aim was to find optimally efficient learning and matched teaching behaviours. The idea was that once these were defined and understood, the pros and cons of each would be circulated, thus enabling teachers to suggest alternative 'better ways' of confronting tasks or tackling problems to their pupils if these were not the ones already in use. As a result all pupils would be enabled to adopt the most efficient problem-solving strategies and the most effective learning would be promoted.

The first step was for teachers to recognise the cognitive style of each pupil and whenever possible match their teaching to that style. This was so that their pupils did not have to make the cognitive shift that would be necessary if they had to embrace another mode. At first glance this would seem to be a tremendous support for children with dyspraxia who would be encouraged to learn and be assessed in the modes that reflected their strengths. These would be likely to be visual and oral learning, rather than written reporting back.

Two of the styles identified by researchers and particularly relevant to dyspraxia are named as:

Reflection —— impulsivity and Field independence —— Field dependence

'Reflection-impulsivity' as a cognitive style refers to the extent to which a child can delay his or her response when searching for the correct answer.

(Meadows, 1993)

Children who make decisions quickly but with many mistakes are said to be impulsive. Most often they will not read any text or listen to any explanation or question carefully enough to be able to give the correct answer. They may be surprised to 'get it wrong' because they have the intellectual capacity to be right. The idea is for parents and teachers to help them understand how their approach spoils their chance of success. Generally speaking, impulsivity is equated with poor results.

Reflective children, however, will study all facets of a task carefully, ponder alternative ways of tackling it and provide well-considered answers which are likely to be correct. The disadvantage of this approach is that it takes time – and there are occasions when time is of an essence and answers must be provided quickly. Endlessly coming up with an alternative way of doing something could mean that nothing ever gets done.

Many children and adults with dyspraxia have a poor concept of time. Timing and pacing do not come naturally. If this is the case, telling the children to 'take more time' or to 'hurry up' may only confuse them, because no one has explained 'how long that much time lasts' and how they are to recognise when that has passed.

There are many variables, however, that confront the assumption that children's results are due to their cognitive style. Perhaps some other activity is more enticing and valuable in the children's eyes so they rush the 'have to do' tasks so that they may enjoy the others. Or perhaps they recognise that no matter how long they spend, they have not the understanding or the necessary skills to complete the task. Perhaps if they have difficulty following a series of instructions – as many children with dyspraxia do – they only complete the one that they remember. This would be likely to be the first or the last. So it is easy for parents and teachers to make errors in their decisions about their pupils' cognitive style.

The second cognitive style that could particularly impinge on the actions of those with dyspraxia is the field independent – field dependent one. Those who are field independent see objects as distinct from their background clearly. This means that spatial judgements, e.g. how high a step is or how far away an approaching bus is, are made quickly and accurately. On the other hand, those who are field dependent have difficulty in making spatial decisions. Misjudgements cause them to trip and fall or to bump into things or people around them. Imagine two boys, one field independent and the other field dependent, playing a game of tennis. The field independent one has a much better chance of winning because he sees the ball coming towards him much earlier and so can move to where it will bounce. This also gives him time to prepare his stance for the return shot. The field dependent child has to wait much longer to see the approaching ball (because it stays as part of the background for longer) and so his return is rushed and often ineffective. To win he has to be that bit more nimble, i.e. he has to take another skill to a higher level to compensate for his field dependence. Much practice is needed, but with perseverance, the children can succeed.

Of course, children do not spend their lives on the tennis courts and so parents and teachers have to know how this will affect other aspects of their children's lives. At the start of the research into these styles, Witkin and Goodenough (1981) considered that field independence was a more helpful trait. More recently, however, the two have been assessed as being different but equally useful styles because field dependent people might just be better at interpersonal and holistic tasks.

Before any conclusion can be drawn there are two further questions to be posed:

- Is cognitive style not task-specific, i.e. do children not change their approach according to the task at hand? Are some of the difficulties associated with dyspraxia caused by this lack of flexibility?
- If they do not make this change naturally, how easy it for those affected to recognise when a different mode would give better results? And even if recognition happens, how possible is it to make the change?

For children who find transfer of information difficult or impossible, finding an alternative way would not seem to be a useful strategy. The fact remains, however, that timing, pacing and spatial decision-making are problematic for many children with dyspraxia. There are other possible reasons for their stumbling and ungainliness which are discussed in the chapter on perception.

Planning and organisation: poor concept of time

Many children with dyspraxia find that this is extremely difficult. Not appreciating how long different tasks take (timing and pacing) impacts on most planning and organisational skills. Spending too long on one thing means the next has to be rushed and if resources have not been prepared due to poor short-term memory, then chaos can result.

Of course this trait, i.e. underestimating the time needed or simply convincing oneself that 'five minutes longer in bed can easily be overcome by missing breakfast', is one shared by many youngsters. But this is a conscious or perhaps semi-conscious decision. The penalties for being late may have been considered and accepted. Children with dyspraxia who are always late are not like this. They genuinely do not appreciate the concept of time.

Poor timing and pacing can affect their movement planning too. If movements are rushed, they tend to be ineffective. Combine this with the effects of a poor working memory which means that the feedback from a previous try cannot help the next and a picture of children 'bumping and barging' and 'falling over thin air' comes as no surprise.

How can this be helped?

Many children find it helpful to construct their own 'task tables'. Ideally these can be laminated timetables with pictures or drawings attached by velcro. If the children draw or cut out pictures from magazines themselves, they can stick them on the timetable and have a visual picture of the key events of their day. When each of these is over, the picture can be removed and kept for another day. Egg timers can help too, for the sand running through gives a visual picture of the 'three minutes' that are left. Laminated 'cues', e.g. 'stay on task' or 'get ready for art now', can act as reminders for the children who have a poor concept of time and save the teacher endless repetitions too.

Not knowing how long to spend on a task and not recognising the amount of detail that has to be remembered means that children with dyspraxia often try to learn/memorise far too much. Students often say they have to work much harder than their friends do, but when it comes to assignments, selecting what they want to say from the mass of detail which they have struggled to memorise can be overpoweringly difficult and so they do not usually receive the credit for all their hard work.

Strategies to help

- Write the title of any assignment and read it ten times.
- Underline the keywords, e.g. 'discuss', 'describe' or 'analyse' and be clear what they mean.
- Write down the word limit and consider how many words should be ascribed to each part.
- Make a visual diagram of the structure of the assignment showing the climax of the 'story' and how many paragraphs come before and afterwards.

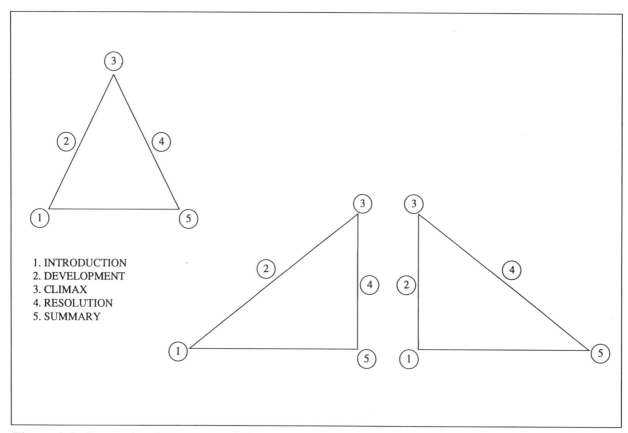

Figure 2.8: Some visual diagrams of the structure of an assignment.

Aids to planning and organising

Because young people with dyspraxia have problems with planning and organisation, it is not difficult to understand why they become so dependent on routine. They have had to work so hard to remember what comes when that any unscheduled activities and last minute changes throw them into confusion. This is because they have lost the markers that help them make sense of their day.

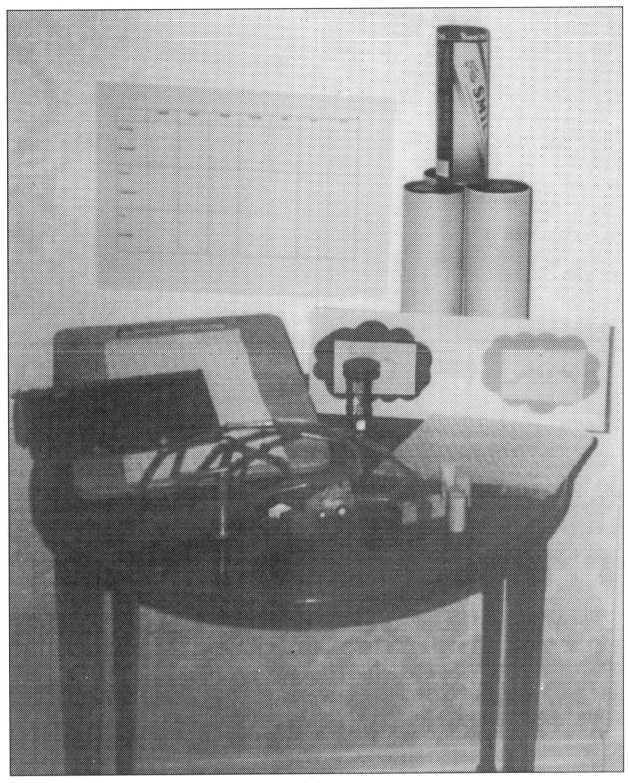

Figure 2.9: A selection of aids to help planning and organising.

Through being involved in devising reminders, the children themselves can help to reduce the effects of having dyspraxia, but expectations have to be realistic and all the interactions positive. In this way they will have the confidence and the competence to learn. The aforementioned list of difficulties, however, explains why there are no immediate 'cures' and why each person must be carefully assessed to ensure that the correct group of difficulties are being addressed.

Chapter 3
Understanding sensory integration and the part the senses play in helping children learn and move

From the moment of birth the child is bombarded with information from the environment. This comes through the different senses (perception), is analysed in the cerebral cortex of the brain (analysis), and then instructions are transmitted to the specific muscle groups that initiate and control movement (action). When this all happens smoothly, i.e. when sensory integration and cross-modal transfer occur (i.e. using one sense to inform another), movement can be dextrous and precise, but if one sense is not functioning properly then the output, i.e. the movement response, can be significantly affected. The importance of the part the senses play in learning to move has been recognised in many schools because they call their early movement intervention programmes 'Perceptual-motor programmes'. What then are the senses and what part does each play in facilitating planned and organised movement?

The sensory receptors are found in the vestibular sense, the auditory and visual senses, the tactile sense, the kinaesthetic and proprioceptive senses, and those of taste and smell. In children with specific learning difficulties, these systems may not be intact. This may cause delay in responding or prevent them giving an appropriate response. Each sense will be considered in turn to explain.

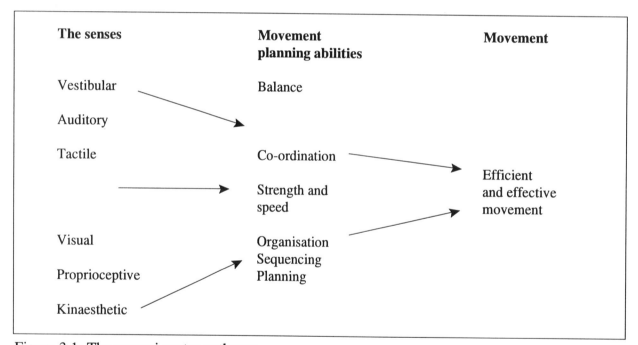

Figure 3.1: The sensori motor pathway.

The vestibular sense

This sense is critically important in maintaining balance. During movement (dynamic balance) and stillness (static balance), the vestibular sense is working to sustain the equilibrium of the body. When the terrain is rough, the body adjusts to prevent falling over and even sitting in a chair needs subtle changes to compensate for reaching and stretching or even slumping if one falls asleep. The vestibular sense is the first sense to 'work' and even before birth it gives the developing foetus directional cues (Goddard, 2002). In children and adults, it controls the adjustments needed when the body changes position. If infection or illness disturbs the system, malaise such as 'swimming head', disorientation or seasickness is felt. This is particularly debilitating because balance is affected. All kinds of sensory information passes through the vestibular system and the brain stem en route to the cerebral cortex. This means that the vestibular system has some influence on the other senses. Their function can be affected if that system is awry.

The vestibular system is located in the inner ear. It has two main parts consisting of three semi-circular canals and two vestibular sacs, all filled with fluid. Each of these is lined by hairs which react to the movement of the body by releasing signals along the cranial nerve pathway. If there is too much fluid sway, motion sickness results and those affected have great difficulty maintaining an upright position.

Many children with dyspraxia have a poor sense of balance. They are also likely to avoid activities that necessitate them leaving the ground, e.g. jumping, climbing and swinging or changing direction quickly, because during these activities their balance would be even more precarious. Often when children are described as being ungainly or clumsy their vestibular system is at fault.

Strategies to help the vestibular sense (balance)

- A soft play area helps children with a poor sense of balance because they can gradually attempt more challenging movements knowing that they are well protected should they fall. Specialist equipment includes padded swings, which move very gently. The children themselves can often control the movement by using their feet to increase or slow down the action.
- Once swinging can be tolerated without distress, movements that tilt the body away from the upright can be introduced, e.g. rolling sideways on a mat then tummy rolling over a large ball (well supported by a teacher).
- A wobble board is fun and the children can have support at first until they have the confidence to try alone. These are useful practices for losing and regaining balance.
- Paddling through shallow water which provides some resistance to the usual walking pattern is a gentle practice and when this is done confidently, striding through waist deep water in a swimming pool can gradually take its place. The deeper water provides more resistance so that the children have a real sense of having to work hard to hold on to an upright stance.
- A rocking horse is ideal for younger children because they can hold on securely as the rocking action happens.

Auditory sense

The cochlea or auditory apparatus is also in the inner ear, sharing the capsule, the fluid and the nerve system with the vestibular apparatus. The two work together and can compensate for one another should one be under par. Children with auditory difficulties may not hear clearly and of course any degree of hearing impairment requires specialist care, for learning language at the correct time is important. There appears to be a critical time when sounds are internalised most easily. Some childhood infections can cause temporary hearing difficulties, e.g. glue ear. Prolonged or recurring bouts may result in the children having difficulty distinguishing between different sounds and this can affect learning to read, spell and write as well as speak. If 'p' and 'b' sound just the same, then 'spelling mistakes' are sure to arise.

Auditory distractibility

As a rule, children with dyspraxia do not have hearing difficulties as measured by an audiologist – they are not hard of hearing – but movements and sounds in the environment can very easily distract them and this breaks their concentration. They have auditory distractibility. As a result their learning suffers. They may also be oversensitive to noises that other children would not notice. Other children passing in a corridor or even leaves rustling outside a window might make these. For noise-sensitive children, these sounds could drown out the teacher's voice. One young girl refusing to go to see a film with her class explained that she would not be able to make out what was said on the screen because other children 'would have popcorn or sweets and the rustling would be all that I could hear'. In a busy classroom it is not surprising that children who hear too much and experience pain in their ears through so doing 'switch off'. This may be a move to help them concentrate on the task they are trying to complete, but though doing this, they miss the next instruction. Teachers often describe some children as 'being in a world of their own'. Perhaps this is the reason why.

Many teachers claim that their children 'don't listen'. Perhaps they really mean that some children cannot listen. This is why listening is now a separate skill to be assessed as a language competence quite apart from talking. In the past it was assumed that if children were not deaf, they were able to listen. Now we know that this is not necessarily the case. Perhaps teachers could speak less so that the children do not have to worry about missing instructions all day long? Perhaps key ones could be introduced by 'Is everyone ready to listen now?' or some other phrase indicating that attention was required and cueing the children that some critical input was about to happen.

Difficulties have to be spotted right away and if the difficulty persists, investigations, ideally with an audiologist or a speech and language therapist, have to be made.

Teachers should also check which is the child's dominant ear, because being left ear dominant could explain a tiny delay in responding. If children are right ear dominant, then the input passes directly to the language centre in the left hemisphere in the brain while sounds from the left ear are transmitted to the sub-language centre in the right hemisphere, through the corpus callosum to the main language centre in the left. While this is almost instantaneous, any minuscule delay can combine with that caused by heavy colds to hamper hearing and delay response time.

Strategies to help the auditory sense (hearing)

- Have the child's desk out of 'traffic' and away from distractions without being isolated, so that auditory distractibility is less of a problem.
- Make sure the child has a clear view of teaching input.
- Keep instructions as short as possible and provide a visual reminder of key points.
- Be sure the children are looking before giving instructions or pointing out directions.
- Use an egg timer or laminated instruction cards to help the child stay on task.
- In a music lesson, use sound maps to give a visual representation with percussion to hold interest and help the children listen.
- Checks on phonological awareness need to be made early so that support can offset difficulties.
- A language centre where the children listen to clear recordings through headphones can allow the children to concentrate on listening. The headphones also help to keep the children in place and help them keep on task.

- Allowing children to wear unplugged headphones can help them concentrate by cutting out classroom bustle.
- Teachers should back up their auditory input with visual if there is a problem. Having a picture book or a text can help compensate for those children who find listening difficult because they are enabled to learn in another mode.
- Teachers could tape-record their own input to find how much teacher-talk goes on. This might just lead to a resolution to curb any unnecessary repetition of instructions.
- Teachers might also investigate whether using a different pitch or more variety in tone made it easier for children to keep listening. Even having different levels of volume in the language centre can test the level children can distinguish sounds most easily.
- Clapping rhythms – simple to complex. Teacher and children take it in turns to clap. When teachers 'get it wrong', children enjoy telling them and repeating the correct rhythm again. This involves lots of listening and using auditory feedback to help the next try.
- Encourage the children to make up phrases using alliteration, e.g. 'the sausage sizzled softly in the saucepan' for the key sound 's' if this is the one not being clearly heard.
- Give the children warning about loud bells or buzzers because these can cause real distress to sensitive listeners.
- Whenever possible avoid using a whistle at games time.
- Set a metronome to a slow speed. Placed beside the child, the repetitive sound can have a calming influence.

At home

- If the children are hypersensitive, turn off the television, especially at meal times.
- Cover hard floor surfaces that reflect sound with a rug, as high heels on wooden floors reverberate sound causing distress.
- Hoover when the children are outside.

Tactile sense

This sense develops early in the first trimester of pregnancy. It provides a safety mechanism allowing the foetus to pull back from any tactile stimulation. This moro reflex, which causes the head to move back and the limbs to extend away from the 'interference', is one of the primitive group of reflexes. It should disappear by two to four months of age. 'If it is retained the children will be oversensitive in one of the sensory channels' (Goddard, 1996). Sudden lights or noises or changes in balance may cause the reflex to act so that the children are always 'ready for action', a state that stimulates the stress hormones. As the children cannot filter out extraneous signals, this hypersensitivity is constantly being reinforced causing the child to be agitated and ill at ease.

Touch receptors cover the entire body although the most sensitive areas are the lips, the mouth and the hands. This explains why babies put everything in their mouths. They are learning about the properties of objects, i.e. their hardness or softness, rigidity or malleability, their shape and smell as well as their taste. Sensitivity in the hands means a quick reaction and so prevents burns or cuts from sharp objects. It also allows gentle, sensitive movements such as stroking a kitten or plucking a guitar string.

Children with dyspraxia are often tactile hypersensitive. Having hair washed or nails cut can cause real discomfort and make these occasions hard to bear. Some children cannot tolerate seams in their socks and parents have to find a supplier of tap dancing socks which have no seams. More worryingly, while some children have phobias about injections and cannot bear their skin to be pierced, they tolerate internal pain too well. Parents have to be extra vigilant in looking out for raised temperatures as signs of illnesses. Other dyspraxic children do not seem to feel the cold at all and will choose inappropriate clothes, e.g. they will happily go out on a freezing day without their coat. This can lead to clothes being left behind and lost because the cold has not reminded the children that they were required.

Some children need firm pressure to make them feel secure. Parents may find that their children only sleep soundly if they are firmly wrapped in a shawl. Light touch may irritate them and the children will shrug it off. If this happens in classroom activities, e.g. in the child refusing to take another child's hand, the hypersensitive child may unwittingly cause offence and be left out of further activities. Teachers today are asked not to touch children at all (because of allegations of abuse), but this can be difficult when the teacher knows that a firm shoulder touch could settle the children and help them feel secure. The area within the brain that registers touch is the somatosensory cortex. This also deals with pain, temperature, pressure and spatial orientation. A less obvious 'job' of the tactile system is to help children learn about directions. When they are touched, they feel where it happens, e.g. to the side or behind or above or below different parts of their body. If edicts proclaim that children must not be touched, they are losing opportunities to develop their spatial orientation.

This combination of effects may explain why it is so necessary to understand the effects of tactile sensitivity. Furthermore, touch is one of the first learning channels to be developed. It precedes both hearing and vision. So its importance as a medium for learning should not be underestimated.

Strategies to help

- Touch a child firmly if at all. Approach from the front so that there are no surprises.
- Sit the tactile sensitive child beside a quiet child and away from 'close encounters'.
- Children are often best at the back of the room so they do not have to worry about what is happening behind them. This also saves them distracting other children if they need to move around.
- Make the child the 'back of the line monitor', i.e. 'in charge', not put there as a punishment.
- A mechanical pencil can last longer before the lead breaks (some children lean too hard and constantly need to sharpen their pencil).
- Allow the children to chew because this is an effective resistive movement, which helps organise the nervous system. If this is difficult within the class, having a 'healthy food' lesson where the children have grated carrots or other hard to swallow food helps. (Check for swallowing difficulties first.)
- Serve drinking water – it is the act of making the mouth function to drink and the swallowing action that helps.

Tactile discrimination: feely bags

These are simply drawstring bags made of dark material (so that the children cannot see through) and large enough to hold four or five small items which have different 'non-sharp' surfaces, e.g. a golf ball, a kiwi fruit, a ball of wool, a pine cone, a pencil sharpener. There are different grades of activity.

- The children guess by feeling, not looking at what is in the bag.
- The children hold one object in their hand and have to retrieve one just the same from the bag.
- The children feel one object within the bag and without taking it out describe it to the other children in their group.
- The children have to feel all the objects then take out the smallest first, then retrieve the others according to size. This helps with size ordering.

Visual sense

Many, even most children with dyspraxia have a strong visual sense and so every opportunity to enable them to learn through this mode should be taken (perhaps they could observe then describe a sequence of events rather then write about them). They should use their visual strength to help them memorise, perhaps through using mind maps. An aerial map of a classroom might also help to compensate for poor body awareness (see also kinaesthetic sense, below) and so prevent knocking into desks or tables and chairs.

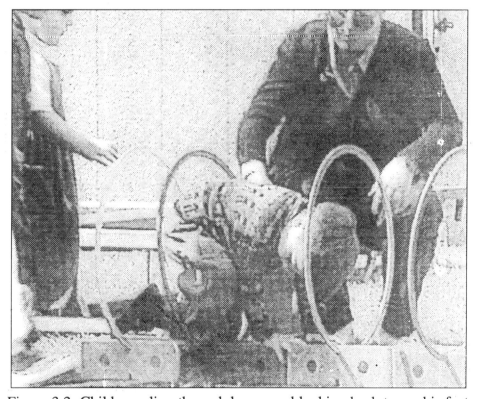

Figure 3.2: Child crawling through hoops and looking back to see his feet.

Visual tracking

Just as the auditory sense does more than control hearing, the visual sense does more than see. It helps maintain balance, i.e. postural control. It is also the key factor in allowing children to track successfully. This skill is required to read words on a page, follow the path of a ball, copy from the board or monitor the route of an oncoming bus. As these activities are carried out, the children learn about distance, i.e. how far away something is, and direction, i.e. where the sound is coming from. Children with poor tracking skills constantly lose their place and may keep using their finger under words while reading when other children of the same age find this unnecessary.

When learning difficulties become apparent, all kinds of vision have to be tested. Maturation of the nervous system should ensure that a complex system of neural connections allows the two eyes to work together to produce a clear and steady image. If children are observed closing one eye to allow them to focus, clearly this is not happening. Sometimes children using two eyes get a blurred or moving picture or see two overlapping letters when just one should be there. If this is the case, then confusion hampers learning to read, pictures acting as visual aids can be distorted and lines meant to guide writing may 'move' adding to the disarray. Children with poor visual discrimination may see letters reversed so they cannot differentiate between 'b' and 'd'. This affects reading, spelling and writing (Miles, 1991).

Visual disturbance can result from an impaired magnocellular system (Stein, 2001). This can cause binocular instability, causing letters on the page to move or cross over each other. Focusing and reading are obviously affected yet the children, not realising that others do not have the same view of the text, blame themselves for not being able to read.

Visual disturbance can also be caused by glare if the children are sensitive to certain frequencies of light spectrum. Some children find they are unable to concentrate in bright light (natural or fluorescent) and sometimes pages with a high level of contrasting colour or busy patterns can swirl or fade. The children just have to look away.

Visual distractibility

Just as some children are distracted by sounds in the environment, other children find it difficult or impossible to cut out visual distracters. Another child waggling a foot, a pencil lying askew on a desk, a curtain flapping at a window – many minor details that most other children would not even notice, disturb and annoy the easily distracted children. Once spotted, the children *have* to move to investigate further. Teachers and parents have to anticipate what could be the cause of distractions and position the children so that they are not in their line of vision.

Early vision

There is continuing debate about how clearly babies see in their earliest days. At ten minutes old babies can copy facial gestures, e.g. putting out a tongue – although the parents' demonstration of this has to last for 60 seconds (BBC Video, 'Baby, it's you!'). This must mean that babies can see clearly enough to copy when they are held at arm's length. This is a clear example of cross-modal transfer occurring between the visual and kinaesthetic senses, i.e. what is seen and what is felt. This is because the babies have not only to watch and recognise what is happening, but then they have to copy by transferring the change of expression to their own face.

Babies can focus both eyes on the same spot, eight inches being the 'best' distance. Within a few weeks they can follow moving objects and by one or two months can discriminate one face from another. Ongoing research from the sixties claims that babies see patterns, i.e. arrangements of facial features, rather than noting each separately and claims that it is recognition of these patterns that encourages them to hold gaze. Perhaps this kind of understanding could be used to promote the recognition of shapes and diagrams in maths and mapping.

Strategies to help 'seeing'

- Coloured overlays and spectacles with tinted lenses reduce glare. The children with these kinds of difficulties must be referred to an ophthalmic optician who specialises in educational colour therapy.
- Reading text that uses justified print can be difficult because the spacing between words has been altered. Reading books where the text has not been justified and that are printed on coloured paper are now available to counteract these difficulties (available from Barrington Stoke Publications, 10 Belford Terrace, Edinburgh, EH4 3DQ).
- Written instructions and visual aids should be as simple as possible as patterns can distort what is seen.

Kinaesthetic sense

The kinaesthetic sense gives a global picture of where the body is functioning in the space around it. It relays information about position and distance so it is fundamental in moving efficiently and effectively. If children see the step further away than it really is, then the movement pattern is going to be affected causing a trip or a fall. Or if the children attempt to join hands in a circle and they misjudge the space between the proffered hands, they fumble and bump rather than moving efficiently without fuss. More worryingly they may misjudge the space between approaching cars or swinging swings and be severely hurt.

Kinaesthetic/proprioception

Proprioceptors are located all over the body in joints and muscles as well as the skin. They provide feedback about the position of the body, i.e. where the different parts are in relation to one another and where the body is in space. The two terms are often used interchangeably; however, used properly the term 'proprioception' refers to the sensations that give 'body position cues' while kinaesthesis specifically monitors movement, i.e. when the muscles contract. Children who have a poor proprioceptive sense may need to move to have their kinaesthetic sense relay positional information. These are the children who fidget and spoil the other children's concentration as well as their own. They can irritate those around them by constantly moving out of their own space and distracting everyone around them. When poor proprioception and poor kinaesthesis come together, the children not only move around but also bump and barge as they go. This may well lead to aggression and fighting.

Strategies to help develop body awareness and spatial orientation

- Games such as 'Simon says' for the young ones.
- Balancing on a wobble board near a wall so that the children have to push away gently. This helps judge distance and pressure.
- The spinning top (see p.13) is excellent for developing awareness of the back. Many children do not feel their backs and so movements that happen behind can be lost. (The top is available from Sales@Rompa.co.uk).
- Teachers should ensure that the 'space vocabulary', i.e. behind, above, in front, below, beyond, to the side, is all understood. This saves confusion in understanding directions.
- Maths activities such as tessellation can help children to be aware of the protruding edges of many shapes and how they fit together. Other puzzles have lifting pegs. These are especially useful for children who are field dependent or who have poor three dimensional vision.

- Moulding clay or squeezing a beanbag can keep the children's hands occupied (they are getting propriceptive feedback) and so help them concentrate on listening.
- The feely bag can be used again, but this time the children have to discern the shapes it holds, e.g. cuboid, cylinder, sphere. Even the nursery children enjoy these 'grown-up words' and should be able to differentiate size with shape.

Smell and taste

These two senses often interact to provide a wealth of information. The fumes of the approaching train can indicate its proximity; while taste can be severely affected by a head cold which affects the sense of smell. Interestingly both smells and tastes can invoke reminiscences and these can be used to encourage memorising and making links between events thus helping transfer of learning. Smells can conjure up multi-sensory images. They can also stimulate taste buds to produce saliva, hence the phrase 'mouth-watering smells'.

Some children can be hypersensitive to smells such as disinfectant and so avoid school toilets, which have just been cleaned. Some will also avoid strong smelling or tasting foods without ever having tried them out while their friends relish curries and other spicy dishes.

It is important to recognise three things:

- Just as the senses work together to interpret the information that comes from the environment and to relay it back to the specific muscle groups which initiate and control the movement, strategies to help develop one sense can be interchanged and substituted to help the other. Whenever possible these should be discussed with the children, e.g. 'Would you like to sit in this quiet space?' for although the teacher has found this move helped one child, the suggestion could distress another.
- No child will be harmed 'by practising the wrong things'. Parents and teachers are often afraid to 'make things worse' and mistakenly assume that they have to know and put over certain 'magic' exercises. This is not so. The aim is for simple practices to be done regularly and to a reasonable standard so that praise can be genuine and the children can recognise that they are making progress. Only in this way can motivation to proceed be 'guaranteed'.
- Intersperse activities with expository teaching. Regular breaks for stretching out – arm swinging back and forwards and across the body or marching round the room – may seem disruptive, but they can help children with movement difficulties to settle. If this is not possible, sending these children out of the room perhaps to take a message to a forewarned secretary allows them to have a 'walking break' and be more able to concentrate on their return.

Most children learn more easily through one sense compared to the others. Teachers have to recognise this and adapt their input to match. Understanding sensory integration is essential, otherwise how are teachers to know that an intricate pattern (which seems colourful and lively to them) appears as a buzzing confusion to some children? Many children have to be helped to overcome a sensory integration disorder so that the information they take from the environment allows them to make appropriate and accurate responses. Teachers have to look specifically at different situations to find when the children have difficulty in using their senses well, e.g. keeping still or tracking from the board, for there are often quite straightforward ways to help. The assumption that children's poor sensory input occurs in every situation is also mistaken. Teachers have to be given time to make a thorough investigation to find what is wrong and to work out the most effective ways to help.

Chapter 4
Observing and assessing movement: knowing how to help

Keen (2001) explains that there is an 80% increase in the number of children presenting with learning difficulties. Whether there are 'more children' or whether adults have become more knowledgeable about specific learning difficulties and are more anxious to push for specialist help is debatable, but the certainty is that many more children need to be helped. The numbers mean that referrals to psychologists and/or physiotherapists may be restricted to only the most severely affected children. While no one would deny them priority, this does mean that special educational needs co-ordinators (SENCOs), support for learning teachers, classroom teachers, nursery teachers and nursery nurses have to be prepared to take on the responsibility of assessing children with movement difficulties and supporting them as they practise and progress.

Many of these practitioners take 'being able to move well' for granted because they have been able to do this themselves. Unless their original training had a major element of physical education, they are unlikely to have studied movement in enough detail to be confident in supporting children with complex difficulties. This may mean that they do not really appreciate what is involved in moving well or know how to analyse what they see. This results in them feeling reluctant or unable to devise the most appropriate ways to support their children. As these skills, i.e. observation, assessment and intervention, are fundamental in observing children to find out if they have dyspraxia and in supporting them when they do, this chapter explains ways in which this could be done.

Observation

First of all, parents and teachers need to look at the children carefully to see if they can cope with whatever they are trying to do. If they can, i.e. if they are competent, the adults need to help them improve through analysing the skill, explaining or demonstrating how it could be done more efficiently and then supervising practice. If the children cannot cope, however, then analysing the movement pattern in terms of the underlying movement abilities, i.e. balance, co-ordination, the use of strength and speed, body and spatial awareness, and finding strategies to help these means that a different set of needs have to be addressed. If the difficulties persist, then specialist help by an occupational or physiotherapist may be required. This would depend on the age of the children, the number of competencies that were defeating them and the level of 'dys' ability they displayed. These professionals would devise and oversee an individualised exercise programme and monitor the progress of each child. In an ideal situation, this would happen in school so causing less disruption to the child's day.

Why is observation of movement necessary?

Being able to move efficiently and effectively in different and changing environments is critically important because apart from the intrinsic enjoyment and confidence that skilled movement brings, it is the fundamental competence in most areas of learning. Today the nature of the curriculum is a practical one. From nursery to university much of the learning is based on problem-solving activities which involve handling materials. In the nursery fine motor skills are developed through threading beads, cutting and spreading at snack, pouring water through syphons and all sorts of activities to develop sensory perception (body awareness songs and jingles) while gross motor skills are developed through outdoor play. In the primary, fixing number cubes, handling basic science equipment, writing stories and participating in team games are just some of the activities added to that list. In the secondaries, handling more sophisticated science equipment during experiments, writing quickly to take notes, and organising and structuring resources to complete assignments all depend on well-developed movement skills. Not being able to do these and very many other movements disadvantages the children and often obscures the competencies they have.

Where should assessors begin?

First of all, adults must assess the children as they move to find if they are competent in the key age-related 'basic' movement patterns, e.g. crawling, walking, running, jumping, grasping and releasing. It is also essential to find whether they can use two hands at the midline of the body doing different things, e.g. writing a letter or opening a jar. These skills are necessary to let them cope at home and at school. The basic movement patterns are so called because they underpin more complex movements, e.g. stepping onto an escalator, running up stairs, catching, throwing and kicking a ball, tying laces and getting dressed/undressed.

Observation naturally leads to assessment and interventions appropriate to the level of competence that is displayed, and so the method of observation must lead to accurate (objective) and comprehensive recordings. Only in this way can the subsequent interventions be the most helpful form of support.

Making observations

Adults carrying out observations have their own preferred ways of doing so – ways that match their own learning style. Some people are particularly analytic and prefer looking for specific points, e.g. incidents of confused laterality or a poor sense of balance across several activities, while others have a natural preference for taking a holistic view of events. This means that they gather a plethora of observations then examine them closely to identify patterns in the data they have amassed. One way is not better than the other, and rich 'finds' can be made by practitioners comparing and contrasting data gathered by each method. The important point is that carefully dated, sequential recordings provide evidence that is much more useful than parents' and teachers' subjective reminiscences.

Observational strategies: sticky label observations

This practice (used in many nurseries) could be continued through school to provide objective dated evidence for older children too. Classroom assistants and auxiliaries could adopt this role. Once these recordings are collated, they are then compared to age-related norms which tell what children of a particular age should be able to do. Movement observations must be made carefully on several occasions in different contexts to pinpoint the children's usual way of moving rather than confusing the picture by focusing on one-off incidents. Observing when the children are unwell or upset or having a first try should be avoided as their competence would be affected on these occasions. 'Clumsiness' may be due to emotional factors or lack of experience, not intrinsic motor disability.

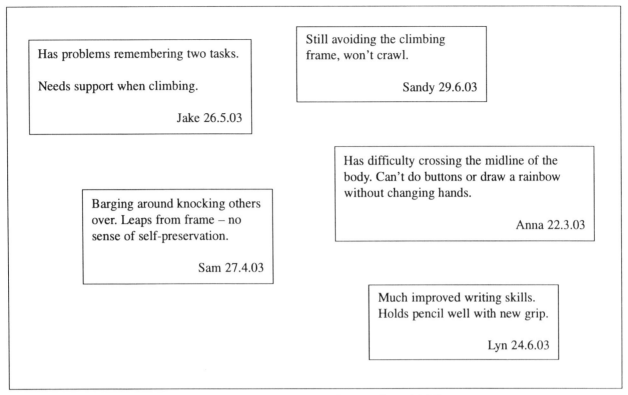

Figure 4.1: Using sticky labels (Source: Macintyre & McVitty, 2003).

Using video as an assessment tool

The transient nature of movement makes observation tricky for it is over in a flash. Observers often wish to share their findings in private without letting the children know they are the focus of attention in case their usual mode of coping is affected. Using a video camera is ideal for this but:

- Written permission from parents has to be requested first.
- The children must be used to the camera so that it does not influence their behaviour or cause them stress.

The film can then be used as a basis for discussion in a staff meeting or, again with the parents' permission, it can provide evidence to get 'outside' clinical testing and advice. A visual image is often clearer than a verbal description or even ticks on a checklist because these can be influenced by the expectations of the observers, the peer group of children who provide the comparisons and the ability of the observers to 'see'.

Observing and recording the children's choices

A first level observation might gather information about the kind of movement activities the children choose and those they avoid. This provides important information because even at age three or four children can self-evaluate and avoid the activities they cannot do.

These observations could be recorded on a time sampling chart which could be used several times if the recordings were carefully dated. Dating allows comparison of results over time and is a very useful way of confirming progress or regression.

Time sampling is useful to get an accurate picture of the things the child chooses to do. The time frame can be adjusted to suit the context but individual observations should be regular and fairly rapid.

Name of child: Amy   Age: 5   Context: Outdoor play

Reason for observation: Checking activities chosen plus social contacts made

9.30	Wanders round outside.	Watches groups but doesn't approach any child.	Decides to go back indoors.
9.32	Tries to get on trike but when trike tips chooses dolls pram. Running action ungainly.	Throws doll on ground and charges pram into the trike.	Darren retrieves doll for her but Amy shrugs him off.
9.36	Staff suggests Amy tries the climbing frame (no other children there).	She runs off avoiding the frame and tries to pull the pram from Darren who had replaced doll.	Shouts 'Give it to me.' Darren very upset and runs to staff who suggest a shared game with the pram. Amy refuses and starts to scream.
9.40	Amy rushes back indoors and knocks a tray to the floor.	Staff take her to dressing up corner.	She calms down listening to music but when Jade and Ian approach she becomes tense again.
9.45	She agrees to have snack and appears to be starving.	The others complain that Amy has all the raisins in her bowl.	She sticks out her tongue and they draw back.

Time sampling can also provide evidence of distractibility – rather then seemingly subjective statements, e.g. 'he can't concentrate.'

Name of child: Alex   Age: 10   Context lesson: Writing a story

Reason for observation: Seeming inability to complete work

10.00	Settles down to begin story.	Appears interested – seems to be confident.
10.02	Searches for word bank book.	Hand up, asks 'How do I spell?'

10.04	Sits down, chews pencil but begins to write.	
10.06	Joins a queue to ask to go out to the loo.	Told to wait till Liam comes back.
10.10	In seat but children passing by window distract.	Teacher asks 'Are you concentrating on the main character now?'
10.11	Alex gets on with his story.	He keeps his head down for 4 mins.
10.15	He has remembered about going to the loo. Before he does this he picks up his paper and puts it in the finished work tray.	Teacher retrieves the paper – on his return five minutes later she praises him for his effort and makes suggestions as to how he might continue.
10.20	Alex smiles pleasantly and wanders out to sharpen his pencil.	Teacher asks Alex to read his story so far to the class.
10.25	Alex takes his story out front and reads confidently – much more than he has written.	The other children know this and giggle – encouraging him to continue.
10.30	Teacher asks how she can put the story on the wall for Parents Night when he hasn't finished writing it down and asks him to complete the work at home.	She anticipates that this won't be attempted and wonders what to do. She knows that Alex can do the work but won't settle long enough – she intends to show his parents this description of his work.

Time sampling sheets like these can spark discussions at staff meetings where helpful strategies can be shared.

Figure 4.2: A time sampling observation chart.

This kind of chart alerts assessors to possible difficulties which then have to be pursued to find if it is lack of interest or lack of skill that is causing activities to be missed. While 'lack of interest' may simply need the activity to be changed, 'lack of skill' pinpoints the area where support is required.

Checklists

Checklists (example in Appendix 3) are best completed when observations from different methods and different observers are collated. They are usually too unwieldy to complete as observations are made, but later collaboration can result in comprehensive lists which can be used as a basis for further planning.

A good checklist will be comprehensive enough to provide a picture of the child across different aspects of development. This is important as these impact on one another (see Chapter 2).

However, a smaller focused checklist may be more appropriate in specific learning difficulties if only one area of development is giving cause for concern.

Within that smaller area, however (and because this text is about dyspraxia, the motor area will be in focus), all competencies should be checked. It is not correct to assume that because gross motor skills are competent, fine motor skills or manipulative ones will be too. Movements of the facial muscles should be checked as well as they are important in many activities, e.g. in articulating speech, in chewing, drinking through a straw, playing some musical instruments and blowing up balloons.

Making observations: setting the scene

Careful planning can help observation sessions to be fruitful. Large apparatus which houses several layers of challenge can be an excellent source of data gathering. However, the observers must have considered:

- the movement patterns they wish to observe;
- whether the challenges suit the children who are to be observed;
- whether the children are to have free choice or to complete a circuit.

The children should know that the apparatus is safe, that mats will cushion any falls and that approach runs have been planned so that bumping and barging is avoided.

Figure 4.3: Apparatus arrangement chosen to allow observation of the basic movement patterns of walking (with turning), crawling, running (with obstacles), climbing, jumping and balancing.

Observing fine motor skills

Observation of these can usually happen more easily indoors. Before the skill is observed and assessed, the same kind of planning needs to happen, i.e. the equipment must not hamper the 'performance'. Writing skills are very often difficult for children with dyspraxia as well as those with dyslexia, but before they are recorded as 'faulty' the height of the children's desks, the steadiness of their chairs and the thickness of their pencils have all to be checked. Even the

54

position of the desk and the paper is important, especially for left-handed children who need more space to the left-hand side and whose work can be cramped by sitting too close to a right-handed child. Many children need a thicker pencil or a pencil grip to help them control their pencil. Those who press too hard often do better with a mechanical pencil which has stronger lead. All of this pre-assessment preparation is necessary if the assessment is confined to the skills it is supposed to measure. It is so easy to have the results biased by other variables.

Many fine motor skills, e.g. threading, sewing, picking up small objects, require precision and dexterity. Within the classroom, fine motor skill difficulties spoil many pieces of work and give a distorted picture of the children's knowledge and understanding. Why should this be?

Sometimes children have little strength in their fingers and strengthening activities such as working with clay can help, while at other times it is lack of hand and finger awareness that causes the problem. Activities where the children look at their fingers, e.g. in playing the piano or action rhymes like 'Incy Wincy Spider', are good to develop this aspect of body awareness/kinaesthesis. (For more ideas see 'Jingle time' published by David Fulton Publishers, London.)

Lack of feeling in the fingers can be gauged by covering the children's hands so that they cannot use their vision to help and touching each finger in turn to see if they can identify which has been touched.

Analysing and assessing movement patterns

First level – 'coping or not coping?'

Careful observation of busy children usually makes it reasonably straightforward to see whether or not they are coping. If they are, if their movement patterns appear 'natural' and competent, they can continue practising or have extensions to provide a greater degree of challenge. Their teachers can confidently claim that the children are competent in the skills that have been demonstrated.

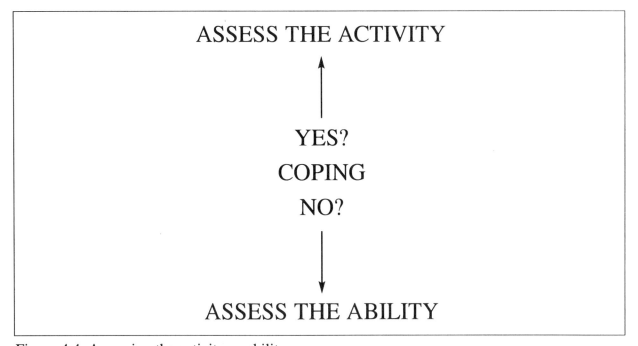

Figure 4.4: Assessing the activity or ability.

Second level – assessing the movement abilities

If the children are not coping, then assessment must move from the activity itself to scrutinising the abilities that underpin the activity. The three kinds shown in Figure 4.5 must all be considered.

Intellectual abilities	Movement abilities	Perceptual abilities
Planning Organising Sequencing	Balance Co-ordination	Visual Auditory
Attending/concentrating	Rhythm and timing	Vestibular
Remembering Following instructions	Use of the correct amount of strength and speed	Kinaesthetic/Proprioceptive
Using feedback	Spatial orientation	Tactile

Understanding and being able to see the effect of poorly developed abilities is necessary if observations are to be recorded accurately.

Gross, fine and manipulative skills

The wide range of movements makes analysing them all an uphill task. However, movement patterns can be subdivided into the three groups identified above.

Gross movement patterns

These patterns use the large muscle groups, e.g. biceps, triceps and quadriceps, to produce a whole body action. During these actions the body usually moves from the spot although sometimes, e.g. in sinking down and stretching up again, it would not. If there is no travel involved, e.g. in waving, these actions are called gestures. Many patterns include travelling at different speeds so this aspect could usefully be included in any assessment. Moving more quickly or turning corners abruptly does require more balance and control but to compensate, the momentum from one movement can help the next part to be completed smoothly.

Children who find balancing difficult will use their arms to help. They may be held in a curling action at the sides.

Motor patterns and observation points

Some gross motor developmental patterns are now given with specific points for observation.

Patterns	Observation points.
Sitting unsupported	Straight back; head held strongly; ability to lean forward and regain balance.
Crawling	Use of the cross-lateral pattern; ability to vary speed; strength in arms/legs; back that is flat, not humping or swaying.
Walking	Poise of body; transfer of weight from heel to toe; smooth fluent action.
Running	Propulsion forward; use of arms to help; strength in both legs to give an even fluent pattern.
Hopping	Transfer of weight to supporting foot; foot dominance; lift helped by arms to give a controlled, balanced action.
Jumping	Strength to leave the ground; control in landing; use of arms to help; unflustered selection of take-off foot.
Skipping	Alternate step-hop pattern; rhythm and flow; control in stopping; head held high.
Sitting and standing still	See important note below.

NB It is important to assess whether children can sit still and stand still, because these are not passive events. The body has to work to stay balanced and controlled to maintain the stillness. Teachers often say, 'But children don't stay still, do they?' implying that this observation is unnecessary or unrealistic. But not choosing to be still is quite different from being unable to be still. For some children this is much harder than moving around. With so much ADHD on the horizon, being able to sit and stand still is a highly desirable competence for children to have. Inability to do so may be caused by a poor sense of balance, difficulty with spatial orientation or inadequate proprioceptive feedback. This needs to be spotted early so that the correct support can be given.

All of these patterns are single ones which should be assessed first.

Transitions

Once skill in single movement patterns has been recorded, combined patterns of movement should be observed. In these, the transitions between the two actions should be such that the flow of the movement is not impaired. If the children can do the single actions, their difficulty often comes 'in between the two parts', i.e. when they have to readjust their weight to begin the second pattern. Children usually achieve combinations of patterns later than the single ones because of the increased demands in both planning and execution. Obviously if the transition is causing the difficulty it would be ineffective to focus on the two parts.

Examples of combined patterns with key points for observations.

Combined patterns	Observation points.
Crawling and reaching out	Overbalancing/collapsing. Shift of weight to accommodate arm stretch. Accuracy of stretch. Hand wavering.
Walking, turning corners sharply	Rounding off corners; disorientation.
Running and jumping	Maintaining the speed. Fluency and control. Smooth transitions. Altering the size of step ready for jump. Amount of strength to achieve height.
Landing	Control and resilience; 'springy knees'.

Open and closed skills

Closed skills are those carried out in a still environment or where the context does not change enough to affect the performance of the action. Repeatedly kicking a ball into the same net or copying a piece of writing from a text lying alongside on the desk or threading beads while sitting at a table would be examples of these. Closed skills are movements that can be repeated exactly. They can be practised, i.e. grooved until they are well done.

But the same basic action as an open skill needs a different kind of competence. When a ball has to be kicked into the net in a team game, the context (the distance, the speed and the approaching defenders) means that the action-plan has to be altered to suit the tenor of the game. Similarly copying writing from the board needs additional tracking skills if it is to be successfully accomplished. Even threading can have added challenges if the beads are of different sizes and wool replaces wire. Swimming in a quiet swimming pool and swimming in a choppy sea where the changing environment needs additional movement competence (balance and spatial orientation) would be another example of the extra demands made by the environment changing a closed skill to an open one.

Practising a closed skill can help the technique of any action but assessors must not assume that because a closed skill can be done well, then success in a changing context is guaranteed. The extraneous demands imposed by the context often deny this. Any assessment, therefore, should look at the same skill in different contexts.

Strategy to help the transfer from closed to open skills

If children are having problems with open skills, then taking them back to check the action as a closed skill can be a very good plan. This means simplifying the context then gradually adding 'distracters' once the skill can be confidently carried out.

Example

Think back to the child kicking a ball into a net. Once this was done satisfactorily as a closed skill, then the child could kick from the same spot with a defender running out without tackling the kicker. The next step could be the child receiving a pass from behind or from the side, lining the ball up then kicking it. Once this was accomplished kicking from various angles could be tried and only then should adding the time pressure of the advancing goalkeeper, which would happen in the real game, be experienced.

Fine motor skills

Fine motor skills use the small muscle groups. They are required in precise movements such as playing the piano, using a computer, lifting and replacing small objects, opening a jar or posting a letter. From this list it can be seen that the hands are the most usual tools and to complete tasks competently, they must be deft and precise.

Hand dominance and confused laterality

Children must also develop hand dominance, i.e. they must know which hand they prefer to use and use it consistently. This may not develop until the age of six (Bee, 1999). Sometimes parents can be misled by thinking their child is ambidextrous when confused laterality, i.e. not knowing which hand or foot to use, is the cause. Children often have to be 'helped to know' by adults watching their efforts done by either hand and asking the child to think about which hand achieved the more successful results. They also may have to be shown how to use the pincer grip and practise releasing whatever they have picked up, especially if they have poor awareness of their hands. Thereafter they need lots of supervised practice to sustain their new skill.

Manipulative skills

Manipulative skills are required when a tool of any kind has to be controlled. Writing and drawing, threading, cutting and stirring, hammering and sawing, using a bat and ball – all of these kinds of activities mean that control has to extend beyond the body itself.

When children find these skills difficult, changing the tool sometimes helps. Providing a softer, smaller ball, a lighter hammer, a needle with a larger eye or a pen with a thicker barrel can often be the solution. If none of these strategies help, however, then exercises to strengthen the shoulders, hands and arms are required.

NB In the past it was assumed that if children's gross motor skills were developing normally, their fine ones would too. Now research is finding that that is not necessarily the case. Children who can sew may not be able to run and jump while those who can do this well, may not be able to form their letters correctly. All aspects of movement have to be checked.

Let us listen to the questions parents, nursery nurses and teachers have asked when they have been baffled by their children's poor motor skills. Let us share some excerpts from the profiles that have been resulted from observations and assessments and find how 'interventions' or strategies to support the children can be put in place. It is important that these activities are fun and/or meaningful to the children – walking along a line with no apparent purpose, will not motivate them at all.

Case study 4.1

First, listen to Graeme's reflection on working with Aaron.

Graeme, a nursery nurse, had noticed that Aaron, aged four, avoided all the construction activities in the nursery. As the child was interested in cars, Graeme had thought that building a garage would be of real interest to him and he suggested they do it together. Aaron knew all about the ramps and what could be wrong with a car, but building a garage was a non-starter. He was not going to do it. He also avoided Lego, woodwork and only occasionally went to the large construction area. What was wrong?

Aaron was avoiding activities that required two hands to work at the midline of the body doing different things at the same time. He had a poor sense of hand dominance, i.e. knowing which hand to use, and if he wanted to draw a rainbow, he started the pattern with one hand and changed his pencil over at the top. Observing Aaron closely also revealed that his shoulder strength was poor – his arms were floppy. This contributed to his lack of control of his pencil so that his writing and drawing were wispy. Being a bright lad he had already, at four years old, self-evaluated his skills to the extent that he avoided activities where he considered he could not succeed.

Graeme's assessment identified poor hand dominance; poor shoulder strength; difficulty crossing the midline of the body.

Graeme's observation and intervention plan

1. Hand dominance
a) Observe Aaron closely to see which hand is used most in a range of activities such as writing, drawing, spreading bread at snack, stirring at baking or making gluck. Find which hand allows the best pencil grip and which results are most pleasing to him. Put a toy equidistant from both of his hands and see which he uses to retrieve the toy.
b) Discuss these findings with Aaron. Be positive. Do not suggest that there is a difficulty; rather ask him to identify which hand gets better results.
c) If he decides that one hand gets better results, gently remind him of this if he later reverts to using the other hand.

2. Working at the midline of the body
a) Work on one hand crossing the midline first.
This is an amended 'Simon says' type of game with the additional challenge of crossing the midline of the body. Body awareness is also helped, e.g.
'Simon says, touch your ear – Simon says, touch your other ear.
As the body has two of most things, this can be repeated using the knees, ankles, eyes, hips, shoulders and elbows. Lots of laughs can follow the children being asked to touch their other nose.
b) While this first activity uses the preferred hand, once competence is shown, it can be extended to using two hands in the same way, e.g.
Use two hands to touch two ears – change them over.
c) Older children enjoy 'Simon says, put one hand on your head and the other one on your foot', i.e. more challenging variations of the same idea.

3. Shoulder and arm strengthening

Strengthening needs the limbs to have some resistance so that they have to work hard. (This is different from mobilising when the important aim is to make the limbs move through the whole range of their possible movement.)

a) Rolling and squeezing firm dough/clay to make different shapes, e.g. snakes, cubes or 'pancakes' which can then be rolled up or plastic cutters can be pressed into the dough or clay to make stars, moon shapes etc.

The dough or clay needs to be at the correct consistency to give some resistance while still being malleable. This activity is useful for older children too. If clay is used, the item can be air-dried to produce a gift to take home. Again squeezing the clay using the fingertips and rolling using the flat of the hand, then rolling the whole amount into a ball to finish, gives good strengthening work for fingers and hands.

4. Hand awareness and strengthening

a) Playing the piano

This is an excellent activity for developing awareness of the hands. Even young children can play a scale of C major and learn to pass the thumb under the bridge made by the other fingers. Simple tunes such as 'Jack and Jill' or 'The First Nowell' can soon be picked out. While the tunes give pleasing feedback, the children are also concentrating on moving one finger at a time. This helps dexterity at the same time as giving them a new skill.

NB A keyboard is not quite so good as the keys do not require the same pressure to play.

b) Passing the 'parcel' – a tube filled with sand

The variation on this old favourite is simply that a wide tube (i.e. suitable for the size of the children's hands – the fingers should not be able to meet) is filled with sand and passed round a circle. The children who all face the centre are not allowed to move their feet and as they are widely spaced, passing the tube means stretching and transferring a weight from one hand to the other. If the tube can be wrapped up in several layers of paper as in the original game, then the unwrapping provides good fine motor skill practice too. The game also develops laterality, i.e. awareness of what is happening at the side of the body.

Case study 4.2

Now Lana, Jake's teacher, explains her concerns:

'Ten-year-old Jake is a loveable lad and quite a clever chap, but life for him is a battleground. He falls over thin air; his knees are always skinned and he constantly bumps and barges so that he is covered in bruises. Just when he has finished a good piece of imaginative writing, he'll spill something over it so that it's spoiled. Sometimes I know he wants to cry and I feel like crying too. Even though he's ten I just give him a hug, but I'm sure that doesn't really help. Sometimes he runs at me to get this hug and he lands up standing on my feet. He's almost as big as I am so it really hurts! What's wrong?'

In her plan for assessment and intervention, Lana explains:

'Jake has two difficulties. His spatial orientation is poor, causing him to misjudge distances between objects (he sees the jar of paint water further away than it really is and so he knocks it over instead of grasping it). The same difficulty causes him to fall. This is because he misjudges the height of a step or the distance between himself and whatever he bumps into!'

'His barging comes from poor judgement of the amount of strength and speed he needs to arrive where he's going. He uses too much momentum and can't stop. Again this comes back to his inability to judge distance.'

Strategies to help

1. First of all Jake needs to practise doing things gently and carefully. He should sit at a solid table that will not tip. The table and chair should be the correct height so that his feet are supported on the floor. This way he does not need to concentrate to hold his balance. He should have an interesting activity such as decorating a birthday card for Mum or a friend. A variety of small objects, e.g. sequins, beads, pieces of lace or doily, strands of cotton, even grains of rice should make this into an original and colourful collage. The action of picking up and placing small items carefully gives the right kind of practice. Speed and strength are no longer required so Jake should learn to use finesse which aids dexterity. Small-scale distances are being judged too.

2. The activity of rolling the ball and catching it before it crosses a line (the line must not be near a wall in case poor judgement of strength and speed causes the child to run too fast and crash into it) is fun and it lets the child see the effect of using different amounts of strength and speed. Jake could try and then immediately evaluate whether more or less strength and speed was required and try again. There is no pressure because there are no other children involved and time is not an issue. Lana had found that 'stand for a moment and check your balance before you begin' was a very useful piece of advice because it allowed time for planning and discussion about what was going to happen. This strategy encouraged using feedback from a previous try too. An important observation about the child's short-term memory could be made here, for some children will not retain what they have practised the day before (see pages *** on memory).

3. For judging distance, strength and speed in a gross motor skill activity, Lana considered that Jake would benefit from jumping practices like this because they would help him to gauge the speed and strength he required. The change of direction would help develop his spatial orientation.

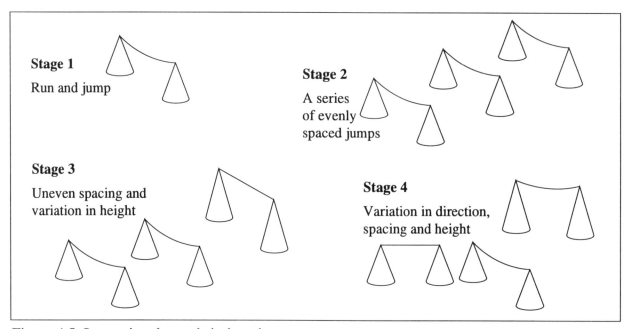

Figure 4.5: Increasing demands in jumping.

This activity can be gradually built up once confidence and competence in each part is gained.

Stage 1: Ask for a straightforward jump over one 'hurdle' and that should be practised on its own – perhaps just varying the height of the jump to add interest until control is gained.

Stage 2: Add other hurdles in a straight line and vary their heights (so that different amounts of strength and speed have to be gauged).

Stage 3: Alter the direction and the distances between the hurdles so that the transitions have to be adjusted on the move.

NB Changing direction quickly can be disorienting for some children so this challenge should be built up gradually. Allow plenty of space for the run up at first, but as skill increases pull the hurdles closer so that the transitions have to be done more quickly. Avoid using canes atop the hurdles as they can be very dangerous if they snap.

Case study 4.3

Hannah is 12 and her dad Alex is losing patience. He asks:

> 'Why does Hannah take so long to do everything? Why can't she hurry up? She has no sense of urgency at all – she's always last to get finished – if she does finish and that's not often. It's easier just to do things myself. The boys were never like this. When she was small we didn't have this problem of having to chivvy her all the time. When we get harassed, she gets upset and then we get upset too. Her teacher says it's the same in school. She says Hannah is easily distracted and although she manages her work to a good standard she rarely finishes what she's supposed to do and this is spoiling her chances of being in the top groups. If she doesn't buck up before secondary, I don't know what we'll do. What's wrong?'

Hannah has poor planning and organising skills possibly due to a poor short-term memory. When she was younger, planning her day was not really her responsibility – in fact her mum now suspects that Hannah, her youngest child, had been overprotected with too much done for her. She realised that in laying out her clothes, preparing her lunch box and always taking her to and from school by car, she had unwittingly removed the need for Hannah to show if she could plan her day. The 'intervention' chosen was that Hannah should gradually assume responsibility for checking that she had her bus pass and take over other 'jobs' around the house to see what she could do.

Ordering resources

Setting the table was Hannah's first task. She had to remember when to do it, then calculate how many of each article was required, then arrange them correctly.

A good 'test' of planning skills is to give a task like this and observe carefully to see how it is tackled. Hannah collected some cutlery and then placed it on the table without finding the tablecloth (which was always used). She made a half-hearted attempt to arrange the cups and plates but then wandered off to watch television and when she was asked why, explained 'I forgot.'

Hannah was distressed by this task. She thought she would not manage it – so the strategy that was put in place was to make a checklist of things to be gathered and arranged. Hannah then ticked off each part as it was completed. At the start this did not hurry things up but it did mean that she gained praise from having completed a worthwhile, helpful task, one that would contribute to her repertoire of useful coping skills.

Other tasks were broken down into smaller pieces too and Hannah soon learned to follow her checklists and complete her task. When she became more confident she explained that when she was given 'a big job to do' she could not remember all the instructions and she panicked. Breaking the task down into manageable bits was 'a very good plan'. She added, 'I don't need to write out checklists now but I still see them in my head and tick bits off as I get done.'

Case study 4.4

Duncan, Simon's classroom assistant, was appointed to try to quell his unruly behaviour in class. Simon is 14 and at the end of his first year in secondary. Duncan tells of his experiences.

'I came into school six months ago to look out for Simon because the staff were worried that he was being bullied and he was obviously so unhappy that school was a nightmare for him. When I arrived he was becoming more and more withdrawn and eventually he refused to do any work at all. To try to help, the school decided to place him in a new class with different children after the holidays so that he could have a fresh start. Unfortunately that doesn't seem to have helped because Simon's attitude changed – over the holidays he became aggressive and pushy. He told me he wasn't going to be bullied any more.'

'In class, he still refused to try to do things like writing stories because he knew his writing was poor. He had had extra writing lessons in the holidays but they didn't help much. Now he has different teachers for different subjects and some of them have run out of patience. After a bit he told me to "Get lost" – and asked what I was hanging around for because I was no use. I was very upset because I had really tried to be his friend but he pushed me away. What's gone wrong?'

Unfortunately Simon's help has come after he has lost his confidence in himself so it will take some time to build up his self-esteem. Duncan had been willing to help but had had no training in how to cope. Once the support for learning teacher took over, she determined to find him a friend. First of all she found his interests – he liked to go fishing – so she chose another boy who was keen on fishing too and they arranged an outing which was successful because of the shared interest. Luckily he lived near Simon so the two youngsters walked to school together. Once the social difficulties were reduced Simon became anxious to learn. This did not happen overnight but once Simon felt he had support and that he had a friend, his demeanour changed and he found school a much more pleasant place to be.

These case studies of children with different aspects of dyspraxia have highlighted the complexity of the condition. The parents and teachers of these children focused on what they considered to be the most debilitating aspects and found strategies to help. The children knew they had difficulties but they also knew that they had the support necessary to reduce their effects. They could begin to look forward more positively than ever before.

Chapter 5
Growing up with dyspraxia

The key messages in this book have been:

- that although dyspraxia does not go away, with support children and adults can be helped to overcome its effects;
- that boosting self-esteem is critically important;
- that this comes through being realistic but consistently positive;
- that different people have an individual profile of difficulties at different levels of severity. This means that parents and professionals have to look beyond any 'label' or diagnosis to assess the whole child;
- that competence can vary from day to day and so assessments have to be made over time and in different environments;
- that the context in terms of the home, the school, the workplace and friendship groups make a significant impact on success;
- that the kind of support, the level of support and the timing of support are critically important although it is never too late to help;
- that the most important people, i.e. those with dyspraxia, will react and respond in different ways due to their temperament, their evaluation of the usefulness of the support and the kinds of activities they see as being important.

This list shows how difficult it is to recognise the interacting difficulties of dyspraxia and offer the right kind of support. Parents sometimes listen to a talk on dyspraxia and say, 'But that's not my child at all!' and they leave disappointed that the strategies that have been suggested to help are inappropriate. They may even wonder whether their child has been given the correct diagnosis (see Chapter 6). Yet others attending the same talk are nodding and agreeing that the picture painted fits their youngster in every detail. They go off refreshed with several ideas that they are anxious to try.

These general talks on dyspraxia are usually based on experiences in helping individual children, yet none of them may be close enough to replicate the pattern of difficulties some children have. Parents naturally 'visualise' their own child as they listen and only want strategies that will help that particular profile of difficulties. At one such talk, one suggestion to reduce the children's stress was that each child could study one subject less at school (one that the child did not relish). Then during that timetabled time the children would be allowed to relax or do any catching up/finishing off or homework. This would save home time for quality family activities that currently are often spoiled by battles to get homework done.

Some parents immediately agreed with this idea, 'for who needs eight subjects anyway?' and most teachers, distressed by having tired, dispirited children in their class, nodded their approval. They considered that being able to do fewer subjects well would be a boost to the children's confidence. One mother, however, explained that for her son, 'being different' would add more stress than it relieved. She explained that despite his difficulties, her son was highly competitive and reducing his timetable would only suggest that he was incapable of doing what his friends did. She acknowledged that he was overanxious and often stressed to a worrying level but she was at a loss to know what to do. 'If he doesn't get top grades in his exams,' she explained, 'he will be inconsolable.' She was emphasising the part the children's temperament plays in evaluating support. She also showed that persistence could result in academic success. Getting the balance between effort and results right, however, is not easy. Suggestions to help each child have to be tempered by understanding how each will respond. This is one reason why parents and teachers and therapists have to work together to understand the effects of their good intentions on the children.

One of the reasons for making inappropriate suggestions for support may be the changing importance of different competencies as the child grows. The change will be caused by:

- the reduction of support from parents in everyday activities of living;
- society's expectation that growing children can make choices and take more responsibility for planning and organising their day;
- the ability/willingness of each child to comply with whatever programme has been suggested.

Changing importance of the key competencies which are often difficult:

Pre-school/Nursery	Primary	Secondary and further/higher education	Employment
Poor muscle tone	Making friends	Social difficulties, immature behaviour	Organisation of self and resources
Inability to crawl	Motor skills, e.g. writing	Planning and organisation	Time management
Poor coping skills	Getting dressed and undressed	Remembering routines/directions	Remembering instructions
Spreading at snack/baking etc.	Games and PE	Following more than one instruction	Choosing a job to suit the skills
Craft activities	Understanding time constraints	Physical activities/leisure choices	Getting a job done in time
Gross motor skills, e.g. climbing, running and jumping	Remembering routines, following rules	Writing skills/ structuring/ sequencing a story	Planning and organising independently
Toileting skills	Paying attention	Judging how much work to do	Driving a car
Judging spaces and distances	Carrying out basic movements well	Getting assignments done in time	Lack of awareness of dangerous situations
Jigsaws and puzzles	Buttons and laces	Carrying heavy bags	Sports skills

How then are the various groups of people affected? Obviously the support and understanding those with dyspraxia receive makes a tremendous difference. In colleges, universities and schools there are resources available. Sometimes a 'label', i.e. a recognised diagnosis, has to precede the acquisition of a laptop or a computer so this is one reason for having a formal assessment. In this age of inclusion, however, when educational policies state that all children should be on a level playing field as they learn, children with specific learning difficulties are entitled to resources to make this happen. Parents can help to make this happen by meeting the staff, explaining their child's difficulties and checking out well in advance what resources will be available. Special equipment often has to be ordered in advance as well as be budgeted for so the more notice the school, college or university has the better. Advance notice also gives the staff time to think through many planning issues, e.g. timetabling rooms so that children with mobility difficulties do not have too far between classes, cloakrooms, lunch rooms and toilets.

Listen now to people affected by dyspraxia and see how their lives have been changed.

Case study 5.1

Aileen and Harry tell of their experiences.

'When Sara was born she seemed to have no muscle tone; she was quite limp. Her head lolled and when we lifted her, her arms hung by her sides. I knew that children with Down's syndrome were low-toned babies, but the doctors ruled that out right away. They told me not to fuss and advised me that the baby just needed time to strengthen up. The muscles in Sara's mouth were affected too. It was so difficult to get her to feed; she couldn't latch on and we were desperate because we thought the food would give her extra strength. I had to dribble the milk gently into her mouth to give her nourishment. Luckily she could swallow all right but it was a constant worry to know if she was having enough food. She was a poor sleeper too and we constantly wondered if she was hungry and so the first 18 months were utterly draining and exhausting.

'She was a year before she sat up without support, she didn't crawl and she was nearly two before she walked, but by that time we could see she was making progress. Her speech was slow too but that wasn't such a worry because we knew she understood everything that was said and her eyes were shining with intelligence. It was a muscular weakness rather than an intellectual one that was holding her back. This affected her feeding too. Getting her to accept solids was a real trial. For a long time she would not accept anything except sieved food. The doctor said it was because the poor muscle tone in her mouth made chewing difficult. Again we had to accept that progress in the motor aspect of her development was going to be slow, but she had such a sparkle that everyone spent time to encourage her. She has a lovely personality. Her social skills and her intellectual ones are a real bonus.

'When it was time for nursery we relied on the teachers to get professional help for us and eventually they were able to have access to a psychologist who diagnosed dyspraxia. The psychologist explained that she didn't usually give a diagnosis before age six because the myelin which surrounds the axons carrying messages to the brain might not have completely built up before then, but in Sara's case she was sure that dyspraxia was there. The staff in the nursery were very interested and provided things like a beanbag to give her a little extra support at story time and they helped her undo buttons and fasten her coat. They were very careful to allow her to choose toys she liked and only gradually encouraged her to try new things. She is becoming more independent now and we have to let her try things for herself even though it can be heartbreaking to see her struggle. We worry how she will cope at primary school though.'

Many children can cope at nursery because of the support they have (the ratio of staff:pupils is higher than in primary schools) and because the curriculum involves learning through play and has much scope for making choices. Furthermore the nursery staff control the routine and check that every child is at the right place at the right time. The children work alone as well as in groups so social skills such as sharing, co-operating and turn-taking may not be well developed in many of the children. In the nursery the space is generally restricted to one or two rooms so finding the way around is not a problem. Moreover, the children do not have to worry about hordes of children milling around at break, often making a great deal of noise. All of these extra demands have to be fulfilled in the primary section. How do children cope?

Case study 5.2

Jon's parents tell of his time at primary school.

'Jon is quick at picking things up and so he was able to read and do his sums with no difficulty. In fact he enjoyed his lessons so much that we had to ask the teacher for "homework" because he wanted to be like his brother Adam – who, needless to say, complained bitterly at having to do it! But we were so dismayed when Adam told us that Jon was always on his own that we went to school to try to find out why. The playground supervisors explained that while the other children were charging around or playing football he stood at the fence and wanted to go back to nursery. They had tried to chat to him but he scowled and wandered off.

'One day Jon came home and said that if we bought him a real leather football then the other children would play with him. Reluctantly we did, but the children just took over the ball and although Jon wasn't told he couldn't play, no one passed the ball to him so he was still left out. He was so miserable because he thought that having the ball would make sure he was in charge of the game.

'The teacher suggested that Jon should practise ball skills so that he was able to join in but by then he had decided he was "no use" and got very downhearted. We reminded him how good he was at reading and sums but Jon now thought that "they're not important!" There is another child in the class with similar difficulties but Jon doesn't want to try to be his friend "because he's hopeless!" So he doesn't get asked to parties and he doesn't want to go to school anymore. He is a sad little boy.'

When things did not improve, Jon's parents took him out of school and contacted Education Otherwise – an alternative means of educating children. Parents who prefer not to send them to school can join this group for support. This was a huge decision and they hope that later on Jon will be willing to give school another try. This answer, of course, is denied to many children whose parents could not or would not wish to cope.

Jon's poor motor skills had affected his social skills to the extent that he could not face school. But what of children who have coped in primary? What effect will the transition to secondary have?

Case study 5.3

Grace is now 12 years old and in her first year at secondary school.

Parent's report

Kate, Grace's mum, explains:

'Over this last year Grace has lost a lot of her vitality and has become quite withdrawn. It's hard to interest her in new activities – she does go along but not by choice. She prefers to stay in her room tape-recording her stories – she has a wonderful imagination. She's a very gentle child, well named as it happens and very biddable but she lacks confidence in herself. I have to say she is slow to get things done – she doesn't seem to understand hurrying up and she is quite clumsy despite being dainty herself which is surprising. Doing up buttons and other fiddly jobs are still very difficult so I buy her clothes and shoes with velcro fastenings to help her.

'I think a lot of her lack of confidence is down to school. When she went there first, she had a lovely teacher who made special timetables for her just to remind her what was happening next, and cards saying things like 'Keep at it, Grace' or 'Pack up your things now – use your checklist' and she was ever so pleased. She brought them home to show us and decorated them with flowers – that took her ages but she was determined to make a lovely job. Unfortunately she left and Grace says that her new teacher just stands in the corridor and shouts and she won't go near her. This is very upsetting and the stress is causing other problems. I've been up to school to explain that Grace needs to get out to the toilet immediately she asks because of poor bladder control, but the teacher still tells her to wait a minute. As a result she comes home wet and I am at my wits' end – in fact I don't think she'll go back after the holidays. She's in the bottom group in all her subjects now – she wasn't before but she is constantly afraid of getting a row, so she is frightened to try anything new. I don't know whether to stick this out and hope that getting a new guidance teacher next year will help or just take her out of that school altogether. Her self-esteem is at rock bottom now.

Teacher's report

'I am Grace's guidance teacher and I also have her for English and I must say I am concerned, for there are lots of times in the day when Grace just switches off and goes into a dream world of her own. She's no trouble in class, in fact she would just sit there all day but she's falling behind all the time. She shouldn't be a low achiever, but if she doesn't listen and follow what's going on, how is she to learn? Whenever I start something new she wants to go to the toilet and misses out and there's just not time to reteach her individually. I have 30 others and some of them have problems too. I think she could have too much done for her at home – she's kept like a little doll and I don't think she's ever had to cope with getting ready or making decisions. She's brought to school and collected and so never becomes involved in any extra-curricular activities where we can relax with the children a bit more or generally in the hurly-burly of school life.

'Her oral language work is very good and in a small group she'll speak out and put forward some lovely ideas. I thought that putting her with children who would listen and follow her plans, that is in a group where she could be a leader, would give her the confidence to speak out to the class, but this hasn't worked yet. She has one main friend and they spend time together, but as far as I can see they don't interact much – just wander around together. The other children tried to make friends, but she didn't respond and they gave up.

'Her motor skills are poor. Her writing is tiny and almost illegible – when I can make it out I am surprised by her insights – she puts forward some interesting ideas – in fact sometimes they become too real to her and she has difficulty separating her stories from reality. Often I would like to praise her more but I worry in case she retreats further. The PE teacher says that because she makes little effort to catch a ball or run in a team game, she gets left out. I do get cross at times because she just appears to tolerate being in school and never shows any sign of being glad to be here.'

The picture painted is that of an unhappy child not fulfilling her potential, but what is wrong? The diagnosis from these two descriptions would point to getting expert help before things got worse. Where should help be sought? Could she have Asperger's syndrome? She is withdrawn, not achieving her potential, yet has a definite talent for imaginative work. Despite this and loving to have stories read to her since she was tiny, her spelling and reading are poor – could she have dyslexia? On the other hand her movement is clumsy and her poor bladder control points to poor muscle tone. From her earlier teacher's efforts to keep her up to speed with reminders, her organisation and planning skills would need to be helped. Could she have dyspraxia? Or has she aspects of different things and if so which should be helped first? How are the parents going to react to the suggestion that their child has a specific learning difficulty which is affecting her learning? Given that they see this as just having emerged recently when the other teacher left, will they blame the school? Is the school at fault for not requesting an auxiliary to help? But that would make the child appear different and there are others in the class needing help too. What is to be done?

Resolving issues like this is always problematic. Getting the parents' permission to make referrals is the first step, because the psychologist should be able to view all the possibilities without being biased and offer some diagnosis. The buddy system where an older child befriends a younger one is ideal for children like Grace who need a helping hand.

Case study 5.3

Adults with dyspraxia

Don, a young adult who had never had any help for his dyspraxia and who as a result had had demoralising experiences in the workplace, explains:

> 'I was so pleased to get a job in a baker's shop. I told Tom – he is the owner – that I didn't have a lot of strength in my arms and he said, "That's not a problem, for I always have two people to carry the breadboards".' Great, I thought! But then I found I had to arrange the cakes in a pattern in the window and place them delicately on glass shelves. I was devastated to find I couldn't do that either. The organisation of arranging cakes was too difficult especially if the shelves were shaky. One day I was trying to put a big meringue in the centre and my thumb went right through it. I paid for it and had it for my lunch but I was so upset that I couldn't carry on. I knew things would just get worse. That sounds pathetic and that's how I felt, so I just left.'

In addition to his spatial planning difficulties, Don found that his fine motor skills were letting him down too. Although he could pick up the cakes, using a pincer grip was not easy and when he managed to grasp them, he found he could not let go so that placing them accurately was beyond his capabilities. Don also had difficulty in judging the strength he needed to deal with fragile things like meringues. In his anxiety not to let the cake fall, he grasped it too hard with disastrous results.

Letting go is often difficult and explains why lots of people cannot throw a ball. They cannot release the ball at the correct moment and so instead of flying into the air, it lands at their feet. Making decisions about the correct amount of strength to use is quite a complicated skill too. Children whose writing is hard and black and those who are forever sharpening their pencils are showing these kinds of tactile difficulties.

At first it would seem that Don had given up too easily but adults with dyspraxia are vulnerable people, just waiting to fail. Don anticipated more 'mistakes' and opted out before they were made. This was extremely disappointing for him and his family. His confidence was shattered once more.

70

Case study 5.4

Shauna, a mum newly returned to the workplace, also had an unhappy experience, this time in an office job. She explained:

> 'First I had to get the mail in and take it round to the different offices. That was difficult but nobody minded when I got a bit lost – in fact I drew a map of where everyone's room was and that helped; at least it did when I remembered to hold it the right way up. But then I had to do photocopying and arrange the sheets of paper into different bundles. No one showed me how to sort them. Eventually I put all the ones with borders in one pile and the plain typed sheets in another. Everyone laughed and I knew they couldn't believe what I had done – I don't know even now what they expected, but I was moved from that job onto filing. That gave me nightmares. I was in such a state by then that I left because there was no way I could manage that.'

One obvious way to help would be for adults affected by dyspraxia to talk through the kinds of jobs they would be able to do, but as Shauna explained, 'How do you know till you've tried?' Don also threw light on the oversimplicity of this suggestion. 'If you've always had dyspraxia,' he explained, 'then you have lived with these difficulties and you forget that it's not like this for other people. Anyway I get fed up making excuses, for that's what it sounds like.' Self-awareness can be poorly developed in some adults with dyspraxia, but this is so understandable if they only discover things they would rather not know. Employers can only help if they appreciate what the difficulties of dyspraxia are and if they have jobs to suit. With time and supervision at the start of a new job, adults with dyspraxia can learn to do many practical things, but it would be best if the intellectual strengths which they undoubtedly have, could be the focus of their job. Then job satisfaction would be more likely to help them stay and make a significant, even outstanding contribution.

Many parents do a great deal of organising for their children to reduce the stress they have in just coping with their day. They have colour-coded charts on the bedroom wall that explain the order in which clothes go on, or show by using pictures attached by Blu-tack on a calendar when gym kit has to go to school. As these children get older they have to be able to cope. Fortunately dyspraxia is being more widely recognised now and this means that schools have to make arrangements to support their dyspraxic children and dyspraxic members of staff.

Case study 5.5

Adults in Higher education

As a child Lyn had been 'forced' to go to dancing and music lessons and resented both activities. 'It was such a struggle to do well,' she explained, 'and I kept having my talented sister held up as an example.' She explained that she always wanted to please her father 'but it took hours of practice – much more than anyone else'. On reflection she considered that 'getting into university to do History was the same thing'. She had had to work and work till she was exhausted.

She claimed that she had two main difficulties. The first was 'not knowing how much work to do' so she attempted to memorise everything on the syllabus, then in the panic of exams could not remember it. The second was 'getting organised so that I could get there in time'. Luckily she had a group of good friends who understood her difficulties and took over practical arrangements like reminding her of when classes were and where they were held.

71

She had wanted to study art but her father had thought history would be more respectable and lead to a better job. Lyn understood his position but resented the stress it had caused her. Now she only wanted to 'get her degree' and then abandon history and look for further training in art.

What kinds of assumptions do those with dyspraxia have to face?

The saddest and most misplaced assumptions that some people make and convey is that because children and adults cannot move well, they have intellectual difficulties as well. They do not recognise that people with dyspraxia do not have global developmental delay. Teachers have to understand and positively endorse both the things the children can do well and give them public praise so that others come to recognise and respect the competencies – often of a high level – that these children have. The difference in IQ status, i.e. between intellectual and performance IQ, however, does mean that people affected by dyspraxia can recognise not only the implications of having it, but the improvement that practice can bring and this can often keep them positive and committed to practising, even when they are very tired with the effort of it all.

Children will often assume that because dyspraxic children are not skilled at games like football, they do not want to play. This means they do not get included. David explained, 'I do want to play and I told them that, but they won't let me be in the team because I can't run fast enough. They said I could be a goalpost and I had to stand with my hands stretched up above my head – for 40 minutes – I wasn't doing that, so I shouted "Get lost" as loud as I could, then I got a row for that as well. It's not fair.' – and it isn't!'

The difference between children who are assessed early and get proper support and those adults who have had to soldier on because 'no one had ever heard of dyspraxia' should be significant. There is no doubt that the interest in dyspraxia is such that professionals will be enabled to help. Parents have new powers and it is hoped that all parents who have children who are not getting the individual support they require and deserve will take steps to make it happen.

Chapter 6
Understanding co-occurrence:
the overlap among specific learning difficulties

As more and more children come forward with or are discovered to have specific learning difficulties, parents can be extremely worried and confused by finding that other children who seem to have the same pattern of difficulties as their own, have been given a different diagnosis. They are concerned that a different label will mean different 'treatment' and that the activities that help other children may be missed by their own. They may also wonder whether the distinction between one named condition and another will lead to an unnecessary sense of isolation. They may even be unsure of what the inherent difficulties in each condition are. For while 'dyslexia' has been around for some time and most parents will recognise that the term primarily indicates difficulties in reading and spelling, dyspraxia is a relatively unknown term, with difficulties that are arguably more pervasive but harder to assess. There is also the question whether movement competence has ever been given the importance it deserves. Many education authorities have tended to concentrate on meeting targets in literacy and mathematics. Perhaps parental pressure has driven this or perhaps not enough people recognised the importance of movement as a contributory factor to prowess in all the curricular skills.

However, in 2003 the importance of movement has been recognised and guidelines to help children with dyspraxia are in every Scottish school. It is critically important that the indicators are recognised and not confused with other conditions or, worse still, not acknowledged at all. (This does not mean that programmes of activities cannot be shared with children to the benefit of them all.)

Parents and teachers are fast coming to the conclusion that, even if a recognised label has been given, the support they offer must depend on the careful and ongoing observation and assessment of each child. This is because the difficulties children have may cross the boundaries between named conditions, i.e. as co-occurring or overlapping difficulties. Parents and teachers have to recognise that each child as an individual, rather than the indicators within a label, must dictate the content of each IEP. One of the recognised dangers in giving a label is that teachers and parents may assume that all the difficulties in each condition are present or are looming, instead of identifying the specific indicators – and the level of each – that each child shows. This could affect their expectations about each child's progress. Alongside any label should come the waiver that the children's difficulties are not static. With support and practice and positive, appropriate teaching, all children can progress.

The diagnostic process can be fraught with difficulties too. Because there are so many more children coming forward without the corresponding number of psychologists, the possibility of referrals is extremely limited. To help, other professionals have to make the assessments. This has resulted in the different groups tending to spot the difficulties that match their own knowledge base first. Some, possibly feeling out of their depth, understandably latch on to a diagnosis that contains these indicators without 'looking beyond the label to see the whole child' (Macintyre & Deponio, 2003). In research to find if this was true, Croll and Moses (1997) discovered that class teachers first identified reading and spelling difficulties and gave a diagnosis of dyslexia. Physiotherapists and teachers of physical education focused on movement difficulties and were more likely to claim that dyspraxia was the difficulty, while those who worked with behaviour difficulties saw the restlessness and distractibility in the children first and diagnosed ADD (attention deficit disorder).

Newton (2002) gives another explanation. He claims that 'the inherent difficulty in classifying children with specific learning difficulties probably reflects the very diffuse and overlapping nature of the spectrum of developmental disorders.' Add to that the fact that children's prowess differs from day to day and it is not so difficult to understand why confusion occurs.

There is also the question as to whether the assessment instruments are comprehensive enough or indeed whether they are appropriate for the job they do. In any 'test' for dyspraxia, it would not be so difficult to observe the execution or doing part (provided the assessor had eyes that could see), because this would concern movement abilities and perceptual abilities, but the underlying planning and organisation is harder to assess. Questions such as, 'Can the children understand the instructions they are given and yet be unable to do the movements that were part of the plan?' or 'Have they the movement competencies but lack ideation, i.e. the capacity to visualise a plan?' need to be asked. If the children cannot do these things, then their movements are going to be limited by factors beyond movement competence itself. All aspects of moving need to be studied to ensure that a comprehensive assessment is made.

To add to the difficulty in making an accurate diagnosis, there are many variables that can affect the assessment, e.g. the test situation, the tester, the previous practice the child has had, the child's body build, to name but a few. Similar concerns affect assessing or measuring progress, for if medication or nutritional additives are recommended, as just two examples, the parents' reliability in offering them, the children's willingness to take them and the 'honesty' in reporting what they did, are all factors that could bias any research findings.

In 2003, researchers are beginning to suggest that the names given to the different conditions are themselves confusing the diagnosis and the subsequent remediation. Yet if individual names were jettisoned, if there were no 'dyslexia' as opposed to 'dyspraxia', parents and teachers would not be given an indication of the key difficulties and surely these should be supported first? Perhaps being told that children had specific learning difficulties and listing the key areas of concern would provide guidance for action while at the same time reinforcing the idea that in all the different named conditions there is a significant overlap, i.e. there are co-occurrent difficulties.

In Canada, where the term 'DCD (developmental co-ordination disorder)' is used in place of dyspraxia and 'co-morbidity' instead of co-occurrence, Kaplan et al. (2001) claim that 'co-morbidity is the rule rather than the exception.' Their statistics show that:

- 33% of those with ADHD also have DCD.
- 52% of those with dyslexia also have DCD.

In London, Keen (2001), a paediatric consultant, has also researched this overlap. She reports that:

- Tourette's syndrome – 60% have ADHD overlap with OCD (obsessive compulsive disorder), Asperger's syndrome and LD (learning disability)
- LD – 30% have ADHD
- ADHD – 30–40% have LD
- ADHD – 50% have dyspraxia
- LD – 50% have dyspraxia
- Autism – 8% have Tourette's

In identifying the shared areas of dysfunction, she sees them as:

- a discrepant cognitive profile
- difficulties in sequencing and ordering

- impairments of social understanding
- executive function deficits, i.e. short-term memory
- focus, adaptation to change

In Edinburgh, Macintyre and Deponio (2003) collated the experiences of many support for learning teachers to find the overlapping skills base.

	Planning & Organisation	Attention Concentration	Short term/ working memory	Inconsistency in responding	Movement fluency	Literacy skills	Delayed language	Confused laterality	Difficulty following instructions	Sensory integration	Social communication	Phonological awareness	Poor concept of time	Rhythmic awareness
	1	2	3	4	5	6	7	8	9	10	11	12	13	14
Dyspraxia	✓	✓	✓	✓	✓			✓	✓	✓	✓		✓	✓
Dyslexia	✓	✓	✓	✓		✓	✓	✓	✓		✓	✓	✓	✓
Asperger's Syndrome		✓		✓	✓	✓	✓		✓	✓	✓		✓	✓
Specific Language Impairment	✓					✓	✓		✓		✓	✓		✓
A.D.H.D.	✓	✓	✓	✓					✓		✓			
A.D.D.	✓	✓	✓	✓					✓		✓			
D.A.M.P.	✓	✓	✓	✓	✓				✓		✓		✓	✓

Figure 6.1: Some key co-occurrent difficulties.

A critical outcome of this is to show how children with different named conditions but with shared difficulties can be helped together in groups thus aiding the children's social development. 'There is no doubt that perceptual-motor programmes (PMPs) help more children than those with dyspraxia' (head teacher of a school where programmes have been part of the everyday curriculum for three years). If competencies like 'difficulty in following a series of instructions' are identified, tasks that give the children time and support to do just that can be built in and practised within each programme. To ensure that this happens, the key learning outcomes have to be clearly identified. These could be that the children should learn to:

1. Carry out basic movement patterns competently, i.e. crawling, walking, running, throwing and catching, writing and handling small objects.
2. Plan a sequence of movement, i.e. be able to say aloud what comes first then next.
3. Use the feedback from one try to improve the next.
4. Organise the resources required for the movement game.
5. Take turns to share equipment.
6. Follow the 'rules' of someone else's game.

Many movement programmes are all about 'doing' activities such as handstands, forward rolls or ball skills. Programmes to nurture the competences in the list 1–6 need to have a wider remit. The teachers have to be sure that the children know and can plan what they wish to do and that they can analyse their attempts. This is necessary if they are to learn to use feedback from one

75

attempt to improve the next. Helping the children to cope with this 'different' aspect of movement competence involves the teacher in discussing and advising but also in following what the children would like to do – at least in the early stages of the programme until the basis of their difficulties is discovered.

Making practice fun

The children must have fun as they practise. They must believe they can make progress. No child should have to anticipate failure or else they will feel defeated before they begin. To achieve this positive ethos, activities should be broken down into small steps so that the children *can* achieve and be awarded genuine praise. One example of a fun activity, which gives lots of scope for observation and assessment, could be:

1. 'Everyone, call out your name. Now call out the first letter of your name!'
   (Teachers assess the clarity of the sound, the speed of the response and attempt to gauge each child's willingness to be involved. If there are children who are hypersensitive to noise then the children can whisper instead of calling out.)

2. 'Now draw the first letter of your name in the air – make it big so that you have to stretch right up to the ceiling and then drop right down to the floor. Now try with the other hand.'
   (Teachers assess the children's balance when they stretch and curl and how easy it is for them to control the whole body movement. If this proves to be too difficult, the children can adopt the crawling position and draw the letter on the floor.)

3. 'Now sit down, lean back on your hands and draw the letter with your toe – stretch it up high – and try the other foot. Watch your toe!'
   (As the tracing happens, teachers should assess the strength in the children's arms through noting whether their arms can support the weight of the body or whether they collapse on the floor. It is also important to observe what happens to the body during the shift in weight bearing which occurs as the toe traces the pattern. The position of hands is important. They should be held quite close to the body with fingers spread out. Strong arms and fingers are needed to help the upper body keep balanced. The tummy muscles have to work very hard too to control the leg action.)

   NB If this is too difficult, the children will not be hurt as they collapse – they can laugh and try again. But this is good strengthening work and also helps body awareness of the different parts.

4. Stand up and hold out the hand that you used – and show me the toe that did the best drawing.
   (Teachers assess and compare hand and foot dominance.)

5. Teacher divides the class into two groups.
   'Now choose someone in the other group. Don't let them know you have picked them. Draw the first letter of their name in the air.' The group sitting out watch to see if they can identify their own letter.

6. The groups change over and the activity is repeated.
   (Teachers assess the identification of another letter and the balance when the size of the drawing is increased.)

This is fun to do. Once the basic patterns are established, the children can draw their whole name or do one letter quickly/slowly or two children can make a sequence, drawing alternate letters of an agreed name. This brings in the challenge of remembering an order and encourages the children to co-operate in twos. It also helps remembering if the activity is developed over several days.

Activity to help organisation and planning

The task is to travel from one end of the bench to the other and then cross over the mat.

The children can select how to do it. They can choose from a variety of small apparatus such as hoops and beanbags, ropes and skittles, bats and shuttlecocks etc. Some children will put obstacles on the bench and step over them (so increasing the balance and spatial judgement demands) while others will set up a more complex arrangement, perhaps adding skittles with canes so that they have to pass under without dislodging the cane.

Teachers ask, 'What are you going to do?' so that the children have to explain their planning (the important part of the activity). At the end of each try, the children should self-evaluate and suggest adjustments either to the equipment or their chosen movements. Emphasis needs to be on simple sequences remembered and done well. Discussions should emphasise space concepts, e.g. 'I'm going *along* the bench, *through* the hoop, *over* the cane, then *under* the rope' or whatever directions the sequence of actions holds.

Once the activity is done the children should be helped to reflect and think about 'what went well and what needs to happen next time.' Usually they enjoy giving themselves a mark out of ten. The mark is not important but it allows the teacher to praise the child then ask, 'Where did you lose that point? This allows the teacher to discuss how the difficulty could be overcome and so develops a partnership approach. The child then tries again. This repetition lets teachers assess if or how well the children can use feedback from one try to help the next.

Activities should be repeated on a subsequent day. This lets the activity improve with practice and it allows the teacher to see how well the sequence has been remembered. A development could be for the children to explain their plan to one another or even teach their sequence to another child. As they do this they use the words, 'first', then 'next' and 'last of all'. This reinforces planning and sequencing.

Using video

This is a very useful strategy especially for children with poor short-term memories for they can use the image to recall activities done earlier. Using film of the second or third tries also shows how much progress they have made. Ideally each child should have their own tape which they can take home or review in private. Soon the children can learn to film each other and 'successes' can be shown to the other children in the class.

The benefits of a daily perceptual-motor programme

In what ways does being involved in a daily perceptual-motor programme help the children? Without fail, teachers report that their children have gained in confidence. Sally, a teacher of seven and eight-year-old children gave, a typical response. She explained:

'When Ross came to school he was a very unhappy child. He lacked confidence in the classroom and he made all sorts of excuses not to go out to play. This was because the other children wouldn't let him join in their games. They told him he was no use – as very young children do. He knew that as far as kicking a ball was concerned, that was true. But after a year on the programme, things are very different. He moves around the classroom confidently and even when he walks in the corridor, he holds his head high. He doesn't shuffle around with his head down any more and he is prepared to give everything a go. He still has difficulties, but being a much happier child means that he doesn't get depressed about them any more. At the programme he made friends with Scott and Liam and they now are responsible for a patch of the school garden. They have a real reason not to play football any more.'

Sally raises the important question of choice. Should young children be able to choose and so avoid the things they cannot do? Or should these things form the basis of practices to improve them? Perhaps the answer lies in the level of difficulty and how long it would take to see an improvement. There are no easy answers. Perhaps it depends on the temperament and the attitude of each individual child. If the relationship between the adults and the children is strong, the children should be able to make their feelings known. They can then make an action plan together – surely the best way of all.

Bibliography

Allport, G. W. (1937) *Personality: A psychosocial interpretation.* New York: Holt.

Ayres, J. A. (1972) *Sensory integration and learning disorders.* Los Angeles: Western Psychological Services.

Barkley, R. A. (1990) 'Attention deficit disorders: History, definition and diagnosis', In M. Lewis & S. M. Miller (Eds) *Handbook of developmental psychopathology, 65–76.* New York: Plenum Press.

Bates, J. E. (1989) 'Applications of temperament concepts', in G. A. Konstamm & J. E. Bates, *Temperament in Childhood, 321–356.*

Bee, H. (1999) *The Growing Child* (2nd Edition). Harlow: Longman.

Berndt, T. J & Keefe, K. (1995) *Friends' influence on social adjustment – Motivational Analysis.* Paper presented at the Society for Research in Child Development, Indianapolis, March.

Bernstein, J. H. (2002) *Assessing the Developing Child: A Neurodevelopmental Perspective.* Paper presented at the British Psychological Society Paediatric Neuropsychology Training Day. Guy's Hospital, London, September.

Bertenthal, B. I. & Campos, J. J. (1994) 'New directions in the study of early experience'. *Child development,* 58, 560–567.

Black, B. (1992) 'Negotiating social pretend play: Communication differences related to social status and sex'. *Merrill-Palmer Quarterly,* 38, 212–232.

Buzan, T. (1993) *The Mind Map Book.* London: BBC Worldwide Publishing.

Caan, W. (1998) 'Foreword', in M. Portwood, *Developmental Dyspraxia, Identification and Intervention: A Manual for Parents and Professionals* (2nd Edition). London: David Fulton Publishers.

Case, R. (1985) *Intellectual Development: Birth to Adulthood.* New York: Academic Press.

Cooley, C. (1962) *Human Nature and the Social Order.* New York: Charles Scribner.

Croll, P. & Moses, D. (1997) *One in five.* London: Routledge and Kegan Paul.

Farnham-Diggory, S. (1992) *The learning disabled child.* Cambridge, MA:Harvard University Press.

Fawcett, A. J. & Nicolson, R. I. (1996) 'Persistent deficits in motor skills of children with dyslexia'. *Journal of Motor Behaviour,* 27, 235–240.

Freedman, D. G. (1979) *Ethnic differences in babies.* Human Nature, 2, 36–43.

Gallahue, D. (1993) *Developmental Physical Education for Today's Children.* Dubuque: Brown Comunications.

Gardner, H. (1983) *Frames of Mind: The theory of multiple intelligence.* New York: Basic Books.

Goddard, S. (1996) *A Teacher's Window into the Child's Mind.* Eugene, OR: Fern ridge Press.

Goddard, S. (2002) *Reflexes, Learning and Behaviour.* Eugene, OR: Fern ridge Press.

Griffiths, M. (2002) *Study Skills and Dyslexia in the Secondary School.* London: David Fulton Publishers.

Harter, S. (1990) 'Processes underlying adolescent self-concept formulation', in R. Montemayor, G. R. Adams & P. Gullota (Eds) *From Childhood to Adolescence: A transitional period?* Newbury Park, CA: Sage.

Henderson, S. E. & Barnett, A. L. (1998) 'The classification of specific motor coordination disorders in children: Some problems to be solved'. *Human Movement Science*, 17, 449–470.

Holt, L. (1991) *Child Development.* London: Butterworth-Heineman.

Howe, M. J. A. (1989) 'Separate skills or general intelligence: The autonomy of human abilities'. *British Journal of Educational Psychology,* 59, 351–60.

Hutenlocher, J. & Burke, D. (1994) 'Why does memory span increase with age?' *Cognitive Psychology,* 8, 1–13.

Jordan, R. & Powell, S. (1995) *Understanding and Teaching Children with Autism.* Chichester: John Wiley.

Kadesjo, B. & Gillberg, C. (1998) 'Attention deficits and clumsiness in Swedish 7-year-old children'. *Developmental Medicine and Child Neurology*, 40, 796–804.

Kagan, J., Arcus, D., Snidman, N., Feng, W. Y., Hendler, J. & Greene, S. (1994) 'Reactivity in infants: A cross-national comparison'. *Developmental Psychopathology*, 30, 342–345.

Kaplan, B., Dewey, D. M., Crawford, S. G. & Wilson, B. N. (2001) 'The term "comorbidity" is of questionable value in reference to developmental disorders: data and theory'. *Journal of Learning Disabilities,* 34 (6), Nov/Dec.

Keen, D. (2001) *Specific Neurodevelopmental Disorders.* Paper presented at the Conference on the Needs of Children with Specific Developmental Difficulties. Bishop Aukland, Feb.

Kirby, A. (1999) *The Hidden Handicap.* London: Souvenir Books.

Kirby, A. & Drew, S. (2003) *Guide to Dyspraxia and Co-ordination Development Disorders.* London: David Fulton Publishers.

Lange, G. & Pierce, S. H. (1992) 'Memory-strategy learning and maintenance in pre-school children'. *Developmental Psychology,* 28, 453–62.

Levine, M. (1994) *Educational Care.* Cambridge, MA: Educators Publishing Service Inc.

Macintyre, C. (2000) *Dyspraxia in the Early Years.* London: David Fulton Publishers.

Macintyre, C. (2001) *Dyspraxia 5–11*. London: David Fulton Publishers.

Macintyre, C. (2002) *Play for children with special educational needs*. London: David Fulton Publishers.

Macintyre, C. & Deponio, P. (2003) *Identifying and supporting children with specific learning difficulties: Looking beyond the label to assess the whole child*. London: Routledge.

Macintyre, C. & McVitty, K. (2003*) Planning a pre-5 setting: An introduction to running a successful nursery*. London: David Fulton Publishers.

Meadows, S. (1993) *The Child as Thinker: The development and acquisition of cognition in Childhood*. London: Routledge.

Miles, E. (1991) 'Auditory Dyslexia', in Snowling, M. & Thomson, M. (Eds) *Dyslexia: Integrating theory and practice*. London: Whurr Publishers.

Mittler, P. (2000) 'Journeys in Inclusive Education: Profiles and reflections', in Clough, P. and Corbett, J. *Theories of Inclusive Education*. London: Sage Publications.

Munden, A. & Arcelus, J. (1999) *The AD/HD Handbook*. London: Jessica Kingsley Publishers.

Nicolson, R. I. & Fawcett, A. J. (1996) *The Dyslexia Early Screening Test (DEST)*. London: The Psychological Corporation.

Portwood, M. (2000) *Developmental Dyspraxia* (2nd Edition). London: David Fulton Publishers.

Richardson, A. (2000) *Dyslexia, Dyspraxia and ADHD: Can nutrition help?* Paper presented at the Durham Conference on Dyspraxia, Durham University.

Robinson, N. (1996) 'Role of the speech therapist', in Reid, G. (Ed.) (1996) *Dimensions of Dyslexia, Vol. 2, Literacy, Language and Learning*. Edinburgh: Moray House Institute of Education.

Scottish Executive (2002) 'Raising attainment of pupils with special educational needs'. Edinburgh: Interchange 67.

Singleton, C. H. (1995) *Cognitive profiling system (CoPS) devised by the Humberside Early Screening research project*. University of Hull.

Sovik, N. & Maeland, A. F. (1986) 'Children with motor problems (clumsy children)'. Scandinavian Journal of Educational Research, 30, 39–53.

Stein, J. (1991) 'Vision and language', in Snowling, M. & Thomson, M. (Eds) *Dyslexia: Integrating theory and practice*. London: Whurr Publishers.

Stein, J. (2001) *Stepping Forward*. Paper presented at the Durham Conference on Dyspraxia. University of Durham, September 2000.

Steinbach, I. (1994) *How does sound therapy work?* Paper presented at the 6th European Conference of Neuro-developmental Delay in Children with Specific Learning Difficulties. Klangstudio Lambdoma, Markgrafenufer 9 59071 Hamm Germany.

Sternberg, R. J. (1986) *Intelligence applied*. New York: Harcourt Brace Jovanovich.

Stewart, R. A. (2002) *Enabling children with Asperger's syndrome to pretend*. Unpublished Masters Thesis: University of Edinburgh.

St James-Roberts, I. & Wolke, D. (1994*) Comparison of mothers' with trained observers' reports of behavioural style in infant behaviour and development,* 7, 299–310.

Tanner, J. M. (1990) *Foetus into Man: Physical growth from conception to maturity*. Cambridge, MA: Harvard University Press.

Thomas, A. & Chess, S. (1977) *Temperament and development*. New York: Brunner/Mazel.

Todd, R. D., Swarzenski, B., Rossi, P. G. & Visconti, P. (1995) 'Structural and functional development of the human brain', in Ciccetti, D. & Cohen, D. J. (Eds*) Developmental psychopathology, Vol.1, Theory and methods,* 161–194. New York: Wiley.

Trevarthen, C. (1997) *Play for Tomorrow*. Video presentation. Edinburgh University.

Wing, L. & Gould, J. (1979) Severe impairments of social interaction and associated abnormalities in children: epidemiology and classification. *Journal of Autism and Developmental Disorders,* 9, 11–29.

Witkin, H. E. & Goodenough (1981) *Cognitive Styles: Essence and Origins*. New York International Universities Press.

Wood, D. (1994) *How children think and learn*. Oxford: Blackwell Publishers.

Appendix 1: Dyspraxia

Although the term 'dyspraxia' is most often used in education, the diagnostic and statistical manual (DSM-IV) of the American Psychiatric Association uses the term 'developmental co-ordination disorder (DCD)' and offers five criteria for diagnosis.

- There is a marked impairment in the development of motor co-ordination.
- The impairment significantly interferes with academic achievement or activities of daily living.
- The co-ordination difficulties are not due to a general medical condition, e.g. cerebral palsy, hemiplegia or muscular dystrophy.
- It is not a pervasive developmental disorder.
- If developmental delay is evident, the motor difficulties are in excess of those usually associated with it.

A summary

Being unable to move effectively and efficiently in different environments impacts on all aspects of daily life. Children find that they are unable to kick a ball, ride a bike or control a pencil, in other words lots of things that they would love to do are denied them and the social connotations of not being able to join in means that friendships are scarce. This leads to lots of frustration and a poor self-esteem. Often the large muscle groups are affected so that the basic movement patterns, e.g. walking and running, are achieved just within the 'normal' timescale but their execution is poor. Sometimes the smaller muscle groups which affect fine motor skills cause difficulties and activities such as writing, being able to chew with the mouth closed and speaking clearly are impaired. Children can find it difficult to know what to do (and therefore to plan their movement) as well as not having the movement abilities, e.g. balance and co-ordination, to carry them out.

Adults who can make more choices about their activities still find that everyday life is curtailed and opportunities for further education and/or employment are reduced. Without help maturation does not do enough to remove difficulties with cutting bread, opening a jar, changing a light bulb, coping with an escalator or carrying a case, to name but a few problem areas. At work difficulties with organising resources, e.g. collating photocopies, packing shelves, designing layouts, all cause problems yet there is no 'intellectual' reason why this should be so.

Constantly feeling clumsy and unco-ordinated can leave people very vulnerable so that they begin to believe they are less useful, even less valuable people. Intervention can help and the new policies on inclusion are there to provide help at any stage of education or in the workplace. People affected by dyspraxia have to know that it is their right to be helped.

Appendix 2: Age-related patterns

Milestones of motor development from age two to six

Age	Locomotor skills	Non-locomotor skills	Manipulative skills
18–24 months	Runs (20 mo.); walks well (24 mo.); climbs stairs with both feet on each step	Pushes and pulls boxes or wheeled toys; unscrews lid on a jar	Shows clear hand preference; stacks four to six blocks; turns pages one at a time; picks things up without overbalancing
2–3 years	Runs easily; climbs up and down furniture unaided	Hauls and shoves big toys around obstacles	Picks up small objects (e.g. Cheerios); throws small ball forward while standing
3–4 years	Walks upstairs one foot per step; skips on both feet; walks on tiptoe	Pedals and steers a tricycle; walks in any direction pulling a big toy; rotates body when throwing but still only uses one arm	Catches large ball between outstretched arms; cuts paper with scissors; holds pencil between thumb and first two fingers
4–5 years	Walks up and downstairs one foot per step; stands, runs and walks well on tiptoe	Boys show mature throwing action	Strikes ball with bat; kicks and catches ball; threads beads but not needle; grasps pencil maturely
5–6 years	Skips on alternative feet; walks a thin line; slides, swings	More children show mature turning and kicking action	Plays ball games quite well; threads needle and sews stitches

(Connolly & Dalgliesh, 1989)

Appendix 3: A developmental record

Child's Name ....   Sex
                                                            Male   Female

Age .... years .... months

This checklist is for one child who is causing you concern. Please record the child's usual level of competence rather than focusing on one unusual occurence. If, however, the child's movement is erratic making a general picture difficult or less than useful, please say that this is the case.

Before looking more specifically at motor development, please say whether you would consider that this was the child's only area of difficulty or whether there are other problems too.

Please tick if appropriate and add any other.

	Yes	No
Does the child have:		
a) Poor sight	☐	☐
b) Low hearing	☐	☐
c) A physical disability	☐	☐
d) Difficulty in understanding instructions	☐	☐
e) Speech difficulties	☐	☐
f) Body build problems	☐	☐
i) very overweight	☐	☐
ii) fragile	☐	☐
iii) little strength	☐	☐
And is the child:		
g) Very tense and unsure	☐	☐
h) Aggressive	☐	☐
i) Lethargic – hard to interest	☐	☐
j) Lacking persistence	☐	☐
k) Seeking attention all the time	☐	☐

Any other difficulty? Please note below.

The checklist below asks you to tick one box for each competence then give a mark out of ten for 'general coping ability' in that field. The categories are 'Yes, can do it'; 'Some difficulty' meaning that the child needs real effort to cope; 'Severe difficulty' meaning that the child does not cope; and 'Regression' which means that the child's performance is getting worse.

NB: This is a movement observation record to help teachers compile Assessment Profiles for school use or for gaining access to specialist help. It is not a test to determine dyspraxia.

Gross Motor Skills

Can the child:	Yes, can do it	Some difficulty	Severe difficulty	Regression	Please give details
a) Stand still, balanced and in control?					
b) Sit still retaining poise?					
c) Walk smoothly and with good poise?					
d) Turn corners efficiently?					
e) Walk on tiptoe with control (count of six)?					
f) Jump (two feet off floor)?					
g) Kick a stationary ball?					
h) Catch a large soft ball when thrown sympathetically?					
i) Roll sideways and recover to stand with a good sense of timing and balance?					
j) Crawl?					

Give a mark out of ten for co-ordination in gross motor skills.

Fine Motor Skills

Can the child:

a) Use a pencil/paint brush with control?

b) Pick up and replace objects efficiently?

c) Use two hands together to thread beads, build Lego or do jigsaws?

d) Draw a person with some detail of parts?

e) Dress in the correct order?

Give a mark out of ten for dexterity in fine motor skills.

Intellectual Skills

Can the child:	Yes, can do it	Some difficulty	Severe difficulty	Regression	Please give details
a) Talk readily to adults?					
Talk readily to children?					
b) Articulate clearly?					
c) Use a wide vocabulary?					
d) Listen attentively?					
e) Respond appropriately?					
f) Follow a sequence of instructions?					
g) Understand					
i) spatial concepts – over, under, through?					
ii) simple mathematical concepts, bigger, smaller?					

Give the child a mark out of ten for intellectual competence.

Social Skills

Can the child:

a) Take turns with no fuss?

b) Interact easily with other children?

c) Take the lead in activities?

d) Participate in someone else's game?

Give the child a mark out of ten for social behaviour.

Emotional Skills

Can the child:	Yes, can do it	Some difficulty	Severe difficulty	Regression	Please give details
a) Appear confident in following the daily routine?					
b) Constantly seek attention?					
c) Disturb other children?					
d) Sustain eye contact?					
e) Cope in new situations?					
f) Appear aggressive or defiant?					
g) Withdraw easily?					
h) Show impulsive behaviour?					

Give the child a mark out of ten for emotional behaviour.

Please give further information below if you feel this would be appropriate. This could concern the areas already mentioned under different topics.

Thank you for completing this.

Glossary of commonly used terms

ABD	A term used by Kaplan et al. in Canada as an umbrella for specific learning difficulties. The term stands for 'atypical brain development' and suggests a biological basis for learning difficulties.
ADD ADHD	Poor attention span affecting concentration. As above + hyperactivity.
APRAXIA	Poor motor planning (praxis). Negative impact on planning a new task.
ARTICULATION	The production of language (vowels and consonants used appropriately and clearly by the active and passive articulators in the mouth) (active: soft palate, lips and tongue; passive: hard palate, teeth).
ASPERGER'S SYNDROME	A specific learning difficulty with the key difficulty of communicating appropriately in different environments.
AUDITORY SENSE/MEMORY	Ability to hear clearly; to discriminate sounds that are similar and different; to hold the sounds in the memory long enough to act upon them in some way.
AUDITORY DISCRIMINATION	Hearing differences between sounds, e.g. 'p' and 'b' thus confusing the meaning in listening to words.
BALANCE	Static balance: the ability to hold the body steady in stillness. Dynamic balance: the ability to be controlled in movement. Dependent on the vestibular sense.
BILATERAL INTEGRATION	The ability to co-ordinate two sides of the body doing similar and different things.
BODY AWARENESS	Knowing through feeling rather than seeing where each body part is in relation to the others and to outside objects (also called body scheme). Poor body awareness causes tripping and general clumsiness.
CLUTTERING	Very quick speech resulting in mumbling. Difficult to understand.
CO-OCCURRENCE	The overlap of symptoms among different conditions, e.g. poor movement in dyspraxia, dyslexia, DAMP and Asperger's syndrome.
CO-ORDINATION	The ability to move efficiently and effectively in different environments. Hand-foot and Hand-eye co-ordination are different competencies – both should be checked.

89

DAMP	Deficit in attention, motor control and perception (Scandinavian term) used for dyspraxia/DCD.
DEVELOPMENT	The changing patterns (physical, intellectual, emotional, social and motor) that occur sequentially in all children.
DIRECTIONALITY	The ability to move in different directions (forwards, backwards, diagonally and sideways).
DISTACTIBILITY	Difficulty keeping on task. Attention span very short.
DOMINANCE	The preferred side used in tasks such as writing, kicking, opening a jar etc.
DYSARTHRIA	A condition affecting speech production resulting in slurred speech due to weak or imprecise movement of the speech organs.
DYSCALCULIA	Poor number and number language comprehension.
DYSGRAPHIA	Poor writing. Difficulty with letter formation (due to fine motor disability).
DYSLEXIA	Difficulty with processing information, particularly reading and spelling.
DYSPRAXIA	A movement learning difficulty. Key symptoms: poor muscle tone/poor movement planning leading to poor co-ordination. Difficulty with new movements, with planning and ordering resources and with the concept of time.
FINE MOTOR SKILLS	The patterns that depend on the dexterity of the small muscle groups, e.g. picking up and replacing an object, writing, computing, speaking, blinking etc.
GROSS MOTOR SKILLS	Movements that require co-ordination of the large muscle groups, e.g. crawling, walking, running and jumping.
HABITUATION	The ability to recall and reuse items stored in the memory automatically, i.e. without detailed planning.
HYPOTONIA	Poor muscle tone allowing too much laxity in the joints making control difficult.
IEP	Individualised education plans for children who need differentiated work.
KINAESTHETIC DEVELOPMENT	Increasing spatial awareness helping efficient movement and directionality.
LATERALITY	Sidedness – competence in using one side of the body more effectively than the other for different tasks.

MATURATION	The inbuilt pattern of age-related changes that happen without teaching and influence what can be done.
MOTOR PLANNING (PRAXIS)	The ability of the brain to organise and plan unfamiliar movements. Essential for sequencing.
MIDLINE	A strong sense of the midline of the body helps movements be balanced as it provides spatial cues (distance and direction). Crossing the midline can be extremely difficult for children with poor hand or foot dominance and for many children with specific learning difficulties, particularly dyspraxia.
PERCEPTION	The brain's ability to make sense of information coming from the environment through the different senses to the brain.
PHONOLOGICAL AWARENESS	Ability to hear the separate sounds within words accurately.
POSTURE PRAXIS	The alignment of body parts during movement and in stillness. The ability to move efficiently and effectively in different environments.
PROPRIOCEPTION	The sensory input from nerve endings in the muscles that relay information about movement – where and how it is occurring.
REFLEXES	Involuntary movement in response to a stimulus and the concurrent physiological process.
REFLEX INHIBITION PROGRAMME	Individual programmes to inhibit primitive reflexes which are hindering the development of postural ones and so preventing fluent co-ordinated movement.
SENSORY INPUT	The passage of impulses from the muscles (proprioceptors) to the spinal cord then the brain.
SENSORY INTEGRATION	The selection and co-ordination of the information (input) coming from the environment (through the receptors in the body to the brain) to produce efficient and effective output.
SEQUENCING	The ability to order steps and stages so that they flow together in the correct order.
SENCO	Special Educational Needs Co-ordinator (England).
SKILLED MOVEMENT	The correct selection of strength, speed and space to provide momentum with control resulting in effective balanced output.
SLI	Specific language impairment. Concerns all children with an abnormality in their grasp of spoken language.
SPATIAL ORIENTATION	The ability to judge distances and directions so that positioning the body in relation to outside objects is secure.

SPEECH AND LANGUAGE THERAPY	Help with eating, drinking, speaking, language and communication difficulties.
TACTILE DEFENSIVENESS	An extreme reaction to being touched or having personal space 'invaded'. A sensory dysfunction.
TONE	Appropriate muscle strength for the task to be done. hyper = too much hypo = too little
VESTIBULAR SENSE	The sense that feeds positional information to the brain. Essential for balanced movement/stillness.
VISUAL SENSE	Allows recognition of people, objects, distances and depths; objects as distinct from their background; parts from a whole object; relationships between people and objects; stimulates hand-eye co-ordination; helps learning by providing visual memory.

Index

Singleton, C. H.   81
Social communication   4, 5, 20, 21, 22, 23, 24, 52, 64, 66, 67, 68, 75, 79, 82, 83, 87, 90
Sovik, N. & Maeland, A. F.   10, 81
Spatial
    – awareness   12, 49, 90
    – orientation   44, 47, 56, 57, 58, 61, 62
Stein, J.   27, 46, 81
Steinbach, I.   81
Sternberg, R. J.   31, 82
Stewart, R. A.   82
St James-Roberts, I. & Wolke, D.   21, 82

T
Tactile sense   40, 43
Tanner, J. M.   26, 82
Temperament   21, 22, 23, 27, 65, 78, 79, 82
Thomas, A. & Chess, S.   21, 82
Todd, R. D., Swarzenski, B., Rossi, P. G. & Visconti, P.   29, 82
Trevarthen, C.   82

V
Verbal dyspraxia   21
Vestibular sense   40, 41, 89
Visual discrimination   46
Visual sense   40, 45
Vulnerability   21, 22, 24, 26, 70, 83

W
Wing, L. & Gould, J.   82
Witkin, H. E. & Goodenough,   37, 82
Wood, D.   31, 82